P9-BZS-316

ROUGH
GUIDES

POCKET **ROUGH GUIDE**
MARRAKESH

ritten and researched by

ANIEL JACOBS

DEC 1 2 2018

princeton

Princeton Public Library
Princeton, New Jersey
www.princetonlibrary.org
609.924.9529

CONTENTS

Clockwise from top: Leather slippers; Mint tea; Majorelle Garden; Koutoubia Mosque

MARRAKESH

The last few years have seen Marrakesh well and truly established as Morocco's capital of chic, attracting the rich and famous from Europe and beyond. Yet the city has always had a mystique about it. It's a place of immense beauty, sitting beneath the dramatic peaks of the High Atlas mountains – its narrow alleys beg discovery while its thoroughfares bustle with excitement and vitality. Arguably the last outpost of the Mediterranean before the Sahara, Marrakesh is still steeped in nomadic and West African influences. Nowhere is this fact more evident than in the Jemaa el Fna, the main square at the heart of the old town. Here you'll find a constant reminder that Marrakesh was once the entrepôt for goods (gold, ivory and slaves) brought by caravan across the desert.

Lantern shopping in the souks

When to visit

Weatherwise, **spring** (March–May) and **autumn** (Sept–Nov) are the best times to visit Marrakesh – it'll be sunny but not too hot. At the height of **summer** (June–Aug), daytime temperatures regularly reach a roasting 38°C, and don't fall below a sweaty 20°C at night, while in **winter** (Dec–Feb) the temperature may reach a pleasant 18°C by day, but it can be grey and even wet; after dark, it's not unusual for temperatures to drop to just 4°C or below. If you come in June or July, you can catch the Festival National des Arts Populaires with its musicians and nightly equestrian "fantasia", while late November or early December is the time to catch Marrakesh's film festival. Expect **accommodation** to be much in demand at Easter and at Christmas, when you should book ahead and expect extra-high prices.

Like all Moroccan cities, Marrakesh is a town of two halves: the ancient walled Medina, founded by Sultan Youssef Ben Tachfine back in the Middle Ages, and the colonial Ville Nouvelle, built by the French in the early twentieth century. Each has its own delights – the Medina with its ancient palaces and mansions, labyrinthine souks and deeply traditional way of life; and the Ville Nouvelle with its pavement cafés, trendy shops, gardens and boulevards.

Marrakesh is sometimes called the Red City, and it won't take you long to see why. The natural red ochre pigment that bedecks its walls and buildings can at times seem dominant, but there's no shortage of other colours – there are few cities as vibrant as this one. Marrakesh breathes the scents of the Middle East and Africa: of spices, incense, and fresh wood being cut and crafted in workshops on the street. Yet simultaneously it oozes a French-inspired elegance in its cool riads, haute cuisine, stylish boutiques and gorgeous clothes. Whatever the wider influences, Marrakesh is first and foremost a Moroccan city, basking in a unique combination of Arab and Berber culture, which infuses its architecture, its craftwork, its cooking and its people.

For visitors, the Jemaa el Fna is undoubtedly the focus, a place without parallel in the world; really no more than an open space, it's also the stage for a long-established ritual in which shifting circles of onlookers gather round groups of acrobats, musicians, dancers, storytellers, comedians and fairground acts. It is always compelling, no matter how many times you return.

Away from the Jemaa, the rest of the Medina is a maze of irregular streets and alleys; losing yourself among them is one of the great pleasures of a visit to Marrakesh. Within the Medina's twelfth-century walls you'll find a profusion of mosques, Koranic schools and *zaouias* (tombs of holy men and women), amid what is, for most Western visitors, an exotic street life, replete with itinerant knife-grinders and fruit sellers, mules bearing heavy goods through the narrow thoroughfares, and country people in town to sell wares spread out upon the ground. The Ville Nouvelle has its own, more modern charms, and beyond it, the Palmery is a little taste of Morocco's date-producing southern desert oases.

What's new

In recent years, some of Marrakesh's traditional crafts have been adapted to create new, contemporary styles, acquiring a chic they never thought they had. So the caftans in Maison du Caftan Marocain (p.47) have been transformed into high-end fashion items, while the humble muds and soaps which people have long used in the

hammam have become the basis for new, exciting cosmetics at shops like Naturom (p.60). Even the cheap old hammam buckets made from recycled rubber tyres have spawned, at shops like Les Enfants de Michelin (p.60), a whole new line in quirky, cool tyre-based accessories.

When you need a break from the bustle of the city streets, you can make for the peaks and valleys of the High Atlas mountains that dominate the city's southern horizon and are just a couple of hours' drive away, where wild flowers dot pastoral landscapes beneath the rugged wildness of sheer rock and snow. In Imlil you can have lunch in a grand old kasbah and walk through gorgeous mountain countryside. At Setti Fatma, you can check out a whole series of nearby waterfalls, or stay in the village for a tajine

and a mint tea right by the gushing river. In season, you can even pop up to Oukaïmeden for a day's skiing.

Also within easy striking distance of Marrakesh, just three hours away on the coast, is the friendly, picturesque walled town of Essaouira. It boasts a completely intact circuit of fairy-tale eighteenth-century ramparts; a beach much favoured by windsurfers; wonderful handicrafts, not least its fine thuya marquetry work; and some great eating places, particularly if you like super-fresh fish.

Minzah pavilion, Menara gardens

Where to...

Shop

The **souk (market) area** in the northern half of the Medina is crammed with little shops selling crafts and clothing, as well as workshops where many of the items are made, and a wander round the souks is one of the highlights of any trip to Marrakesh. Before setting off into the souks, it's worth taking a look at the Ensemble Artisanal, or a fixed-price shop such as Entreprise Bouchaib, to get an idea of quality and prices. Parts of the souk, and other locations in the Medina, specialize in specific items: **carpets** in the Souk des Tapis, for example; **babouches** (Moroccan slippers) in Souk Smata; and **lanterns** in Place des Ferblantiers. Other specialities include **Morocco leather**, which is cured in the local tanneries, and local **clothes**, some of which are targeted particularly towards Western tastes. For **wooden marquetry**, Essaouira is the place to go. In most places, of course, you'll have to **haggle** (see box, p.117).

OUR FAVOURITES: The olive stalls p.30, Moulay Larbai p.48, Les Enfants de Michelin p.60

Eat

The most atmospheric place to eat is at the food stalls on the **Jemaa el Fna**, right in the middle of the action, but if you don't fancy mucking in at street level, you can find several decent, moderately priced restaurants overlooking the square. Inexpensive café-restaurants are concentrated in the streets just south of the Jemaa, and scattered around the **Medina** are some excellent upmarket palace-restaurants, usually with a floorshow in the evenings. These are often hidden away, and can be difficult to find, especially at night – if in doubt, phone in advance and ask for directions; sometimes the restaurant will send someone to meet you. Most of the city's French-style cafés, bistros and restaurants, many of which are very good, are in the **Guéliz** district in the centre of the Ville Nouvelle, where there's a smattering of restaurants offering cuisine from further afield too. Only the more expensive places in the Medina serve **alcohol**, but in the Ville Nouvelle all but the cheapest places are licensed.

OUR FAVOURITES: Dar Essalam p.62, Al Fassia p.72, Winoo p.76

Drink and go out

As an almost entirely Muslim city, Marrakesh doesn't have a big drinking culture. **Bars** tend to be either chic and sophisticated or rough and low-life (these can be fun, but for men more than for women), and there's not much in between. Most bars are in the Ville Nouvelle, with much more limited choice in the Medina. The city does have some quite decent **nightclubs**, all of them in the Ville Nouvelle, and mostly attached to five-star hotels. They play a mix of Western and Arabic music, but it's the latter that really fills the dancefloor.

OUR FAVOURITES: African Chic p.76, Theatro p.79, Taros, Essaouira p.93

Marrakesh at a glance

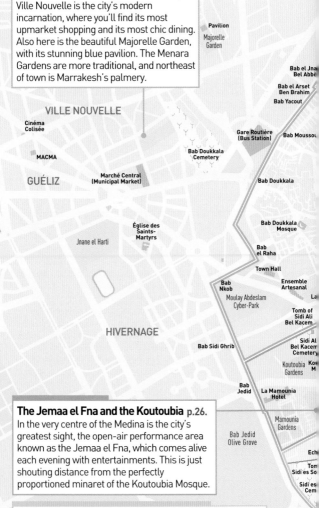

The Ville Nouvelle and Palmery p.64.
Beyond the city walls, the brash and busy Ville Nouvelle is the city's modern incarnation, where you'll find its most upmarket shopping and its most chic dining. Also here is the beautiful Majorelle Garden, with its stunning blue pavilion. The Menara Gardens are more traditional, and northeast of town is Marrakesh's palmery.

The Jemaa el Fna and the Koutoubia p.26.
In the very centre of the Medina is the city's greatest sight, the open-air performance area known as the Jemaa el Fna, which comes alive each evening with entertainments. This is just shouting distance from the perfectly proportioned minaret of the Koutoubia Mosque.

The Southern Medina and Agdal Gardens p.52.
The old city's southern half – which includes the Mellah (Jewish quarter) and Kasbah (citadel) – is home to the awesome ruins of the El Badi Palace, the magnificent Bahia Palace, and the beautiful Saadian Tombs. To the south, the Medina gives way to the Agdal Gardens, Marrakesh's largest area of greenery.

Pavilion
Majorelle
Garden

Bab el Jna
Bel Abbè

Bab el Arset
Ben Brahim

Bab Yacout

VILLE NOUVELLE

Cinéma
Colisée

Gare Routière
(Bus Station)

Bab Moussou

Bab Doukkala
Cemetery

MACMA

GUÉLIZ

Marché Central
(Municipal Market)

Bab Doukkala

Bab Doukkala
Mosque

Église des
Saints-
Martyrs

Bab
el Raha

Jnane el Harti

Town Hall

Bab
Nkob

Ensemble
Artesanal

La

Moulay Abdeslam
Cyber-Park

Tomb of
Sidi Ali
Bel Kacem

HIVERNAGE

Sidi Al
Bel Kacem
Cemetery

Bab Sidi Ghrib

Koutoubia
Gardens

Ko
M

Bab
Jedid

La Mamounia
Hotel

Mamounia
Gardens

Bab Jedid
Olive Grove

Ech

Tom
Sidi es So

Sidi es
Cem

The Northern Medina p.36.

The old city's northern half is the Medina at its most labyrinthine and atmospheric. You'll find the main souks here, where crafts are made the traditional way and sold in specifically dedicated areas. Top tourist attractions include the exquisite Ben Youssef Medersa and the unique Almoravid Koubba, not to mention the city's insalubrious but fascinating leather tanneries.

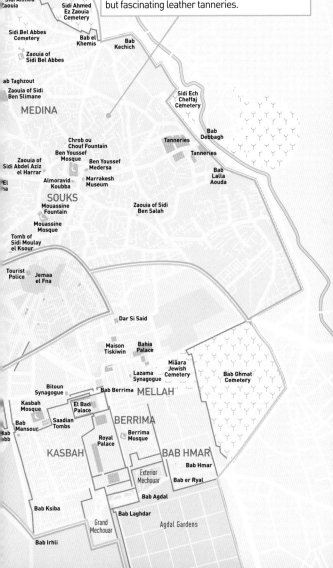

Sidi Ahmed Zaouia

Sidi Ahmed Ez Zaouia Cemetery

Sidi Bel Abbes Cemetery

Bab el Khemis

Bab Kechich

Zaouia of Sidi Bel Abbes

ab Taghzout

Zaouia of Sidi Ben Slimane

MEDINA

Sidi Ech Cheffaj Cemetery

Bab Debbagh

Chrob ou Chouf Fountain

Ben Youssef Mosque

Tanneries

Tanneries

Zaouia of Sidi Abdel Aziz el Harrar

Ben Youssef Medersa

Almoravid Koubba

Marrakesh Museum

Bab Lalla Aouda

El na

SOUKS

Mouassine Fountain

Zaouia of Sidi Ben Salah

Mouassine Mosque

Tomb of Sidi Moulay el Ksour

Tourist Police

Jemaa el Fna

Dar Si Said

Maison Tiskiwin

Bahia Palace

Miâara Jewish Cemetery

Lazama Synagogue

Bab Ghmat Cemetery

Bitoun Synagogue

Bab Berrima

MELLAH

Kasbah Mosque

El Badi Palace

Saadian Tombs

BERRIMA

Bab Mansour

Berrima Mosque

bb

Royal Palace

KASBAH

BAB HMAR

Exterior Mechouar

Bab Hmar

Bab er Ryal

Bab Ksiba

Bab Agdal

Bab Laghdar

Grand Mechouar

Agdal Gardens

Bab Irhli

15

Things not to miss

It's not possible to see everything that Marrakesh has to offer in one trip – and we don't suggest you try. What follows is a selective taste of the city's highlights, and ideas for trips further afield. All have a page reference to take you straight into the Guide, where you can find out more.

> **Essaouira Gnaoua Festival**
> A celebration of music from the unique Sufi sect originally formed by slaves from West Africa.

< **Jemaa el Fna**
The heart and soul of the city, and an absolutely unmatchable experience after nightfall.

∨ **Tajine**
Slow-cooked until sumptuously tender, Morocco's signature dish is served at any cheap diner, but it's best at top-class restaurants like *Al Fassia* (see p.72).

< Haggling in the souk
p.36 & 117

Haggling is de rigueur in the souk, and while you may initially be nervous, it's actually very sociable and rather fun.

∨ Thuya marquetry
p.89

Essaouira is the place to buy items made from the wood and root of the thuya tree, often inlaid with other woods.

< Almoravid Koubba
p.40
Morocco's only surviving
Almoravid building shows how
many typical motifs originate
with this dynasty.

**∨ A calèche ride through
the palmery**
p.67
What could be more tranquil of
an afternoon than a peaceful
ride through the date palms in
an old-fashioned horse-drawn
carriage?

∧ Ben Youssef Medersa

p.40

A medieval Koranic school where you'll find the city's finest examples of tilework, stucco and carved cedarwood.

< The Koutoubia

p.28

The ultimate masterpiece of Almohad architecture, perfectly proportioned and breathtakingly beautiful – the city's emblem.

∧ **Majorelle Garden**
p.64
One of the world's great gardens,
created by a French artist in the
early twentieth century.

∨ **Festival National des
Arts Populaires**
p.122
Singing, dancing, camel racing
and an equestrian "fantasia"
feature in this week-long festival
in June or July.

∧ El Badi Palace
p.56
Morocco's most fascinating ruin, the remains of a huge, rambling palace with pavilions and formal gardens.

‹ Staying in a riad
p.97
The best places to stay in Marrakesh by far are these lovely old houses with internal patio gardens, lovingly restored in traditional style.

< **Maison Tiskiwin**
p.52
A unique collection of artefacts harking back to the days of the trans-Saharan caravan trade between Morocco and Mali.

∨ **Skiing at Oukaïmeden**
p.82
Twenty kilometres of runs for skiers and snowboarders in the snowy High Atlas mountains, two hours from town.

Day one

Jemaa el Fna p.26. Start out from Marrakesh's main square, just as it gets going in the morning.

Souks p.36. Make for the souk area north of the Jemaa, where Marrakesh's vibrant markets are concentrated.

Place de la Kissaria p.40. Pay a visit to the Marrakesh Museum, and have a look at the Almoravid Koubba while you're passing.

Ben Youssef Medersa p.40. The most impressive medieval Koranic school in Morocco, with zellij tilework, intricate stucco and finely carved cedarwood.

🍴 **Lunch p.50.** *Le Foundouk* is housed in an old caravanserai, and is now a stylish restaurant.

The Tanneries p.43. Head east to the stinky tanneries, checking them out at ground level and then from a roof terrace.

Zaouia of Sidi Bel Abbes p.44. Go past Chrob ou Chouf fountain to the *zaouia*, or tomb, of Sidi Bel Abbes, the most important of Marrakesh's "Seven Saints".

The Majorelle Garden p.64. Leave the Medina for the Ville Nouvelle's most important sight, a wonderful ornamental garden with cacti and lily ponds.

🍴 **Dinner p.74 & p.79.** Dine on the city's top Italian cuisine at *La Trattoria*, amid Bill Willis's beautiful decor. Later, you might head to *Theatro* for some dancing.

Juice stall, Jemaa el Fna

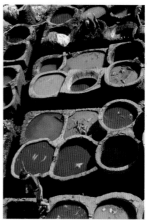

The Tanneries

The Majorelle Garden

Day two

Bab Agnaou p.58. Begin at Marrakesh's most magnificent city gate, featuring concentric arches and fine carving. It also has a patisserie right inside it.

The Saadian Tombs p.58. Arrive early to avoid the crowds (the enclosure opens at 9am) so you can appreciate the exquisite tombs at their best.

Place des Ferblantiers p.53. Head to Place des Ferblantiers to watch the metalworkers beating out decorative lanterns by hand.

El Badi Palace p.56. Take some time to explore this extensive and extremely impressive ruin, with its sunken gardens and pavilions.

Bab Agnaou

🍴 **Lunch p.61.** Pause at the *Café el Badia*, where you can opt for a cheap set menu and get right up close to the storks nesting on the walls of the palace.

The Bahia Palace p.53. This nineteenth-century grand vizier's palace contains some of the city's finest painted ceilings.

Dar Si Said p.52. Stop off at this nineteenth-century mansion, now a museum, to admire the woodwork and costumes.

Jemaa el Fna p.26. The Jemaa el Fna should now be warming up for the evening, with snake charmers giving way to storytellers and musicians.

El Badi Palace

🍴 **Dinner p.33 & p.49.** Have supper at the food stalls on the Jemaa. Afterwards, head to the *Café Arabe* for a drink.

Bahia Palace

ITINERARIES

Marrakesh's souks

In the medieval Medina, every craft had its own souk, or market, where artisans wrought and sold their products – a tradition that continues today.

Souk Smarine p.36. This is the souks' main thoroughfare, where shafts of sunlight through the slatted roofs dapple the street below.

Rahba Kedima p.37. An open square whose apothecary stalls sell all manner of strange traditional cosmetics.

La Criée Berbère p.37. Once the site for slave auctions, this covered area now specializes in rugs and carpets.

The Kissaria p.37. The covered market at the very heart of the souks, where clothes and fabrics dominate.

🍴 **Lunch p.51.** Dine on Moroccan dishes with a modern twist up on the terrace of the *Terrasse des Épices*, with views across the rooftops.

Souk Smata p.45. Also called the Souk des Babouches, this is where the slipper-makers ply their wares. Benzarrou Jaâfar offers traditional designs for men and women.

Souk Haddadine p.40. The ironworkers' souk is a cacophony of clanging as the craftsmen hammer out their metal.

Souk Sabbaghine p.37. Here in the dyers' souk, plain wool is boiled up in vats of luridly tinted liquids and hung out to dry across the street and the rooftops.

🍴 **Dinner p.50.** Try *La Maison Arabe* for a really top-notch Moroccan meal in elegant surroundings.

Souk Smarine

La Criée Berbère

Ironworker, Souk Haddadine

Indulgent Marrakesh

Marrakesh is Morocco's indisputable capital of chic, so there's no better place for a spot of pampering.

Breakfast at the Patisserie des Princes p.31. Set yourself up for the day with coffee, croissants and maybe even a pastry.

A calèche ride in the Palmery p.67. Sit back in a horse-drawn carriage and ride in style through Marrakesh's oasis.

Ice cream at Oliveri p.71. Pop into this elegant salon to eat the city's best ice cream in old-fashioned style.

Shop in the Ville Nouvelle p.68. Check out fine antiques, home furnishings and sumptuous Moroccan leather.

 Lunch p.73. Head to the *Grand Café de la Poste* for fine international cuisine in a classic restaurant.

Get a henna tattoo in the Jemaa el Fna p.26. Have your hands decorated with the same designs as a Moroccan bride.

Mint tea at La Mamounia p.31. Take tea on the terrace and enjoy the royal gardens.

A steam bath at Les Bains de Marrakech p.103. Book the full package, with steam bath, massage, mud packs and all the extras.

 Dinner p.34 & p.73. Have supper at *Le Tobsil*, where the pastilla and the couscous are second to none. Advance booking is essential. Then pop into the *Comptoir Darna* for a post-prandial cocktail.

Mint tea, La Mamounia

Ice cream, Oliveri

Les Bains de Marrakech

A food tour of Marrakesh

Marrakesh is a superb place to sample the very best of Moroccan cuisine, be it aromatic couscous, succulent tajines or a cinnamon-dusted pastilla pie.

Café-Restaurant Toubkal

p.31. Set yourself up for the day with a mint tea and *msimmen*, a chewy, pancake-like bread that's Morocco's answer to an Indian paratha.

Mahalabat Qasab es Sukar

p.31. As the day hots up, refresh and rehydrate yourself with a delicious glass of freshly pressed sugar cane juice, or a *msimmen*.

Herboriste la Santé **p.46.**
Browse the enticing variety of spices – both medicinal and culinary – on sale in the Rahba Kedima.

Olive stalls **p.30** Taste some of
Morocco's myriad types of olives at this little souk dedicated to them.

Mahalabat Qasab es Sukar

🍴 **Lunch p.32.** Try out Marrakesh's own popular speciality, *tanjia*, right by the olive souk at *Hadj Mustapha*.

Amal Restaurant Solidaire

p.72. Book yourself a cookery workshop at this excellent women's centre which specializes in developing catering skills.

Amandine **p.71.** Sample the
lovely little macaroons with a coffee at this elegant café-patisserie.

Al Jawda (Chez Mme Alami)

p.71. Treat yourself to a box of mouthwatering little almond pastries at this tip-top Moroccan cake shop.

Olive stalls

🍴 **Dinner p.72.** Dine on excellent Fassi cuisine at *Al Fassia* including pastilla and a choice of succulent lamb tajines. Advance booking is wise. For dessert pop into *Oliveri* (see p.71) for an ice-cream.

Tajine at Al Fassia

Religious Marrakesh

A deeply pious city, Marrakesh is steeped in Islamic learning, and boasts an array of mosques, Koranic schools and Sufi zaouias, with a few churches and synagogues too.

Église des Saints-Martyrs p.66. The city's main Catholic church, dedicated to six Franciscan friars executed here in 1220.

Zaouia of Sidi Bel Abbes p.44. A *zaouia* (Sufi centre) built around the tomb of a twelfth-century saint who is the patron of Marrakesh's blind people.

Zaouia of Sidi Abdel Aziz el Harrar p.42. This Sufi shrine is dedicated to one of the city's famous "Seven Ssaints".

Ben Youssef Medersa p.40. In Marrakesh's oldest, most beautiful Koranic school, take a break from admiring the architecture to check out the students' quarters upstairs.

Tiles on Ben Youssef Medersa

 Lunch p.51. The *Terrasse le Medersa*, upstairs in an old *fondouk*, close by the Ben Youssef Medersa, is a handy spot for lunch, with views of the medersa roof.

The Koutoubia p.28. While admiring the minaret, take time to look at the ruined foundations of the original mosque, since rebuilt to face Mecca properly.

Kasbah Mosque p.58. Come to see how the main mosque of the citadel quarter has been restored to look as it did in its heyday.

Zaouia of Sidi Bel Abbes

Lazama Synagogue p.56. Like many of the Mellah's synagogues, this is also a private house; the main Jewish cemetery is nearby.

 Dinner p.62. Treat yourself to a palatial meal at *Dar Essalam*, where you can admire the superb architecture and enjoy entertainment from Andalusian-style musicians.

Dar Essalam

PLACES

Carpets for sale in the Medina

The Jemaa el Fna and the Koutoubia

Once, every Moroccan city had a main square where storytellers and musicians entertained the townspeople, but the Jemaa el Fna has always been the biggest and most important, drawing the greatest variety of performers, and it remains Morocco's single top attraction. To see why, come here as it gets going in the evening; you'll soon be squatting amid the onlookers, soaking in the unique atmosphere. For respite, the café and restaurant rooftop terraces set around it afford a view over the square and of the Koutoubia minaret – as much a symbol of Marrakesh as Big Ben is of London – while the northern edge of the square marks the beginning of Marrakesh's souks, or markets.

Jemaa el Fna

MAP p.28, POCKET MAP A12–B12

Nobody is entirely sure when or how the Jemaa el Fna came into being – or even what its name means. The usual translation is "assembly of the dead", which could refer to the public display here of the heads of rebels and criminals, since the Jemaa was a place of execution well into the nineteenth century.

By day, most of the square is just a big open space, in which a handful of **snake charmers** play their flutes at cruelly de-fanged cobras, **medicine men** (especially in the northeast of the square) display cures and nostrums and **tooth-pullers**, wielding fearsome pliers, offer to pluck the pain from out of the heads of toothache sufferers, trays of extracted molars attesting to their skill.

Jemaa el Fna at night

It isn't until late afternoon that the crowds really build. At dusk, as in France and Spain, people come out for an early evening **promenade** (especially in Rue Bab Agnaou), and the square gradually fills with storytellers, acrobats and musicians (see box below), and the crowds who come to see them. Most of the spectators are Moroccan of course (few foreigners, for example, will understand the storytellers' tales), but tourists also contribute to both the atmosphere and the cashflow. There are sideshow attractions too: games of hoop-the-bottle; **fortune-tellers** sitting under umbrellas with packs of cards at the ready; and women with piping bags full of **henna** paste, ready to paint hands, feet or arms with "tattoos". These will last up to three months, but beware of synthetic "black henna", which contains a toxic chemical; only red henna is natural.

For **refreshment**, stalls offer freshly squeezed orange and grapefruit juice, while neighbouring handcarts are piled high with dates, dried figs, almonds and walnuts, especially delicious in winter when they are freshly picked in the surrounding countryside.

As dusk falls, the square becomes a huge **open-air dining area** (see box, p.33), packed with stalls lit by gas lanterns, and the air is filled with wonderful smells and plumes of cooking smoke spiralling up into the night.

Performers in the Jemaa el Fna

The locals' favourite among the square's performers are the **storytellers**, great raconteurs who draw quite a throng with their largely humorous tales, though of less interest to non-Arabic speakers of course. Also in attendance are **acrobats** and male **dancers in drag**. In the daytime, monkey men and snake charmers encourage tourists to pose for photos, but the animals are poached from the wild and treated cruelly, and paying for photos encourages this. Far better then to have your picture taken with the **tooth-pullers**, or the **water sellers** in their magnificent red regalia.

Dozens of musicians in the square play all kinds of instruments. In the evening there are full groups including **Gnaoua trance-healers**, members of a Sufi brotherhood of Senegalese origin, who beat out hour-long hypnotic rhythms with clanging iron castanets and pound tall drums with long curved sticks. Other groups play Moroccan popular folk music, known as *chaabi*, and late into the night, when almost everyone has gone home, you'll still find players plucking away at their lute-like *ginbris*.

RESTAURANTS

Al Baraka	9
Chez Bahia	16
Chez Chegrouni	5
Earth Café	22
El Bahja	21
Hadj Mustapha	2
Hotel Islane Terrasse Panoramique	15
Jemaa food stalls	7
Jnane Mogador	20
Kassabine Café	1
Le Marrakchi	6
Le Tobsil	3
Les Prémices	13
Pizzeria Portofino	14
Restaurant Argana	4
Restaurant Oscar Progrès	23
Taj'in Darna	10

ACCOMMODATION

Hotel Aday	8
Hotel Afriquia	3
Hotel Ali	2
Hotel Central Palace	4
Hotel CTM	1
Hotel de Foucauld	11
Hotel Gallia	12
Hotel Ichbilia	6
Hotel La Mamounia	13
Hotel Medina	5
Hotel Sherazade	10
Jnane Mogador Hotel	7
Riad Zinoun	9

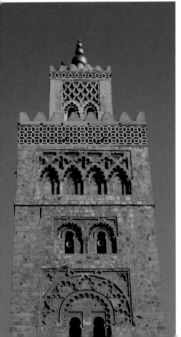

The Koutoubia

MAP ABOVE, POCKET MAP F6

Rising dramatically from the palm trees to the west of the square, the **minaret** of the Koutoubia Mosque – nearly 70m high and visible for miles – is the oldest of the three great towers built by Morocco's twelfth-century Almohad rulers (the others are the Hassan Tower in Rabat and the Giralda in Seville). The minaret's proportions give it an extraordinary lightness of feel, and its 1:5 ratio of width to height set the standard for minarets throughout Morocco. Indeed the Koutoubia displays many features that are now widespread in Moroccan architecture – the wide band of **ceramic inlay** near the top, the castellated **battlements** rising above it, the *darj w ktarf* ("cheek and shoulder" – similar to the French *fleur de lys*) – and the

The Koutoubia

Map labels

The Jemaa el Fna and the Koutoubia

Tomb of Sidi Moulay el Ksour
PLACE BAB FTEUH
SOUK QESSABINE
RUE DABACHI
RUE DABACHI
DERB HAJRA
DERB JAMAA
RUE DES BANQUES
RUE KENNARIA
Tourist Police
PLACE JEMAA EL FNA
Cinéma Eden
RUE RIAD ZITOUN EL JEDID
N
PLACE FOUCAULT
Calèches
Buses
AVENUE EL MOUAHIDINE
RUE MOULAY ISMAIL
RUE BAB AGNAOU
RUE TETOUAN
RUE BEN MARINE
Hammam Sidi Bouloukate
Hammam
DERB SIDI BOULOUKAT
Forex Bureau
DJAMA
Cinéma Mabrouka
DERB SIDI BOULOUKAT
DE LA RECETTE
DERB EL LAKHDAR
DERB EL ZOUINA
DERB SSATHA
RUE ZITOUN EL QEDIM
Hammam Polo
Petits Taxis
Asni Shared Taxis
RUE CASBAH BEN NAFAA
RUE LALLA RAHA
RUE BIN KHALDOUN

| 0 | metres | 150 |
| 0 | yards | 100 |

BAR
Grand Hotel Tazi   1

SHOPS
Boutique Bel Hadj   1
Hermane Rahal   4
Jemaa el Fna market   3
Olive stalls   2

CAFÉS
Aqua   8
Café-Restaurant Toubkal   11
La Mamounia Terrace   24
Le Grand Balcon du Café Glacier   12
Mahalabat Qasab es Sukar   18

PATISSERIES & ICE CREAM
Oriental Legend   17
Patisserie des Princes   19

---

alternation of patterning on the different faces. At the summit are three great **copper balls**, thought to have been made originally of gold.

Originally the minaret was covered with plaster and painted, like the Kasbah Mosque, near the Saadian Tombs (see p.58). In the evening, the minaret is floodlit to stunning effect.

To the north of the present-day mosque (which only Muslims may enter), you can see the remains of the original mosque, which predates it. The excavations confirm that the mosque had to be rebuilt to correct its alignment with Mecca.

The Koutoubia gardens

MAP ABOVE, POCKET MAP E6–F6
Av Houman el Fetouaki. Daily 8am–6pm.

To the north, south and west of the Koutoubia are the Koutoubia Gardens, attractively laid out with pools and fountains, roses, orange trees and palms. Something of a focus for promenading Marrakshis, they give excellent views of the Koutoubia.

La Mamounia hotel and gardens

MAP ABOVE, POCKET MAP E6–F7
Av Bab Jedid.

It's worth popping into Marrakesh's top hotel for a pot of tea on the terrace (see p.31) and a look at the opulent interior, with its 1920s Art Deco touches. The terrace overlooks the hotel's **gardens**, which regular visitor Winston Churchill described to Franklin D. Roosevelt when they were here together in 1943 as the loveliest spot in the world. Originally laid out by the Saadians, they retain the traditional elements of citrus trees and walkways. You'll have to dress up to see them, however, as jeans, shorts, trainers and T-shirts are all banned.

Shops

Boutique Bel Hadj

MAP p.28, POCKET MAP B11
22 & 33 Souk Fondouk Louarzazi, Place
Bab Fteuh ☎ 0524 441258. Daily
10am–5pm.

If silver is your thing, this shop
on the north side of Place Bab
Fteuh is the place to look, with
heavy silver bracelets from around
Morocco and as far afield as
Afghanistan, sold by weight and
purity. There's other silverware
too – antique teapots for example
(often as not made in Manchester
for the Moroccan market), along
with tea trays.

Hermane Rahal

MAP p.28, POCKET MAP A13
3 Rue Moulay Ismail ☎ 0661 162535.
Daily 10am–10pm.

Should you wish to buy a ceramic
tajine (see box, p.34), this
unassuming little store is the place

Olive stall

to do it. There are pretty tajines
here from Fez and Safi, but the
real McCoy are the heavy red
earthenware jobs which hail from
Sale on the coast, where the local
clay is perfect for the purpose.
A Sale tajine will set you back
20–70dh, depending on the size.

Jemaa el Fna market

MAP p.28, POCKET MAP B12
East side of Jemaa el Fna. Daily 9am–9pm.

Just off the big square is this small
covered market, of most interest
as a place to get fruit and veg,
though it also sells meat and even
shoes. Handy if you're staying in
one of the small hotels south of
the Jemaa.

Olive stalls

MAP p.28, POCKET MAP B12
Souk Ableuh. Daily 10am–8pm.

Located in a little square just off
the Jemaa el Fna is a row of stalls
with olives piled up at the front.
The wrinkled black ones are the
typical Moroccan olive, delicious
with bread but a bit salty on their
own. As for the green olives, the
ones flavoured with bits of lemon
are among the tastiest. Other
delicacies include spicy red *harissa*
sauce and bright yellow lemons
preserved in brine, the brine
taking the edge off the lemons'
acidity.

Cafés

Aqua

MAP p.28, POCKET MAP B12
66 Pl Jemaa el Fna ☎ 0677 710417.
Daily 10.30am–12.30am.

Cool, modern surrounds, and
two terraces overlooking the
western side of the Jemaa el Fna.
There are espressos made with an
imported Italian coffee blend, as
well as sandwiches, salads, juices
and pizzas, but the location and
ambience are more interesting
than the food.

Café-Restaurant Toubkal

MAP p.28, POCKET MAP B12
Southeast corner of Jemaa el Fna, by Rue
Riad Zitoun el Kedim. Daily 24hr.

As well as fruit juices, home-made
yoghurts and pastries, they offer
a range of salads, tajines and
couscous here. It's also a great
place for a breakfast of coffee
with bread and jam or *msimmen*
(a chewy, flat griddle bread) with
honey. You'll be hard pushed to
spend more than 70dh.

La Mamounia Terrace

MAP p.28, POCKET MAP E6
Av Bab Jedid ☎ 0524 388600,
Ⓦ mamounia.com. Daily 10am–7pm.

Dress up in proper shoes, and a
skirt or trousers, to try the poshest
cup of tea in town, served on the
terrace of the *Hotel La Mamounia*
(see p.29). The tea itself is nothing
special, but it does allow you to
check out the hotel's interior, and
its beautiful gardens.

Le Grand Balcon du Café Glacier

MAP p.28, POCKET MAP B12
South side of Jemaa el Fna, next to the
Hotel CTM. Daily 10am–10pm (food served
until 8pm).

This is the place for the fullest
view over the Jemaa, taking it
all in from a perfect vantage
point, but it isn't as close-up as
the *Restaurant Argana*. You can
come up for just a drink (tea,
coffee or soda) but they also do
food, including salads, pizzas
and tajines, with most dishes at
50–65dh.

Mahalabat Qasab es Sukar

MAP p.28, POCKET MAP B13
38 Rue Bab Agnaou. Daily 7am–11pm.

This may be a standard coffee and
juice bar at the back, but out front
they sell "crêpes" (well, *msimmen*)
stuffed with various sweet and
savoury fillings for 5–12dh, and
wonderful freshly pressed sugar

Patisserie des Princes

cane juice (6dh a cup) – the first
place in Marrakesh to sell it. Look
for the juice machine as the sign is
in Arabic only.

Patisseries and ice cream

Oriental Legend

MAP p.28, POCKET MAP B12
Rue Bab Agnaou ☎ 0524 420320.
Daily 10am–9pm.

The Marrakesh branch of a well-
established Agadir ice-cream
firm offers a gimmicky range of
flavours, including Oreo, Bounty
and After Eight, as well as fig,
date and even licorice – heaven
on a scorching day. From 8dh, but
takeaway only.

Patisserie des Princes

MAP p.28, POCKET MAP B13
32 Rue Bab Agnaou ☎ 0524 443033. Daily
6am–11pm.

Patisserie des Princes is a sparkling
place that sells mouthwatering
pastries at prices that are a little
high by local standards but
well worth the extra. They also
have treats like almond milk and
ice cream. The *salon de thé* at
the back is a very civilized place
to take a continental breakfast,
morning coffee or afternoon tea.

Restaurants

Al Baraka

MAP p.28, POCKET MAP A12
1 Pl Jemaa el Fna, by the Tourist Police
☎ 0524 442341, ⓦ albaraka-marrakech
.com. Daily noon–3pm & 7–10.30pm.

This is a cool outdoor space serving tasty meals (*menus* 320–450dh) accompanied in the evening by a belly-dancing show. Not in the same league as some of the more palatial Medina restaurants, and something of a tourist trap, but the food's good, the surroundings pleasant and the location couldn't be handier. Licensed.

Chez Bahia

Chez Bahia

MAP p.28, POCKET MAP B12
206 Rue Riad Zitoun el Kedim ☎ 0677
169209. Daily 8am–midnight.

A café-diner offering pastilla, low-priced snacks and excellent set breakfasts with pancake-like *msimmen*. For the rest of the day, there are wonderful tajines bubbling away out front to tempt you. You can eat well here for 60–80dh.

Chez Chegrouni

MAP p.28, POCKET MAP B12
Northeast corner of Pl Jemaa el Fna
☎ 0661 434133. Daily 11.30am–midnight.

Popular with tourists, this place does decent couscous and good tajines at moderate prices (mostly 65dh a throw, with vegetarian options at 45dh), though the portions are on the small side. Come at a quiet time if you want to bag one of the seats on the upstairs terrace overlooking the square.

Earth Café

MAP p.28, POCKET MAP B13
1 Derb el Zouaq, off Rue Riad Zitoun el
Kedim ☎ 0661 289402,
ⓦ earthcafemarrakech.com. Daily
11am–10pm.

Marrakesh's first vegetarian restaurant offers nine dishes (at 70dh a throw), of which five are vegan. Choices include veggie burgers, "warm salad" and filo pastry parcels containing various combinations of vegetables and sometimes cheese. The portions are generous, and the food is well prepared and delicious, enough to tempt any carnivore – all in all, it's a nice change from the usual Moroccan fare. They also serve excellent juices and herbal infusions, and the atmosphere is intimate and relaxed. The café has another branch at 1 Derb Nakous, off Rue Road Zitoun el Jadid.

El Bahja

MAP p.28, POCKET MAP B13
24 Rue Bani Marine ☎ 0524 440343.
Daily noon–11pm.

This place, whose patron has appeared on a British TV food programme, is popular with locals and tourists alike. It's good value, cheap and generally unexciting, though its kofta is highly rated and don't miss the house yoghurt for afters. Set menus 70–80dh.

Hadj Mustapha

MAP p.28, POCKET MAP B12
Souk Ableuh ☎ 0661 344341. Daily
10am–10pm.

One of a trio of cheap, hole-in-the-wall diners selling tanjia, the most quintessential of Marrakshi dishes (see box, p.34) – this is where working-class locals come to eat it. If you drop by in advance, you can have it cooked to order.

Hotel Islane Terrasse Panoramique

MAP p.28, POCKET MAP A12
279 Av Mohammed V ☏ 0524 440081.
Daily 7am–11pm.

The main attraction at this rooftop restaurant is its unparalleled view of the Koutoubia rather than its not-very-good-value set menu (120dh). That said, its breakfast buffet (55dh) isn't bad.

Jnane Mogador

MAP p.28, POCKET MAP B12
Jnane Mogador Hotel, Derb Sidi Bouloukat
☏ 0524 426323, ⓦ jnanemogador.com.
Daily 7.30–11am (for breakfast) &
noon–10.30pm.

Non-guests at this little hotel are welcome for breakfast, lunch or dinner. Tuck into a tasty set menu (90–150dh) with couscous or tajine in the roof terrace restaurant, and round it off with a relaxing glass of fine mint tea. The service is every bit as good as in places charging twice the price, and it's a very handy bit of respite from the hustle and bustle on the streets below.

Jemaa food stalls

Marrakesh's tourist guides often suggest that the Jemaa's food stalls (open daily from dusk until 11pm; map p.28, pocket map B12) aren't very hygienic, and it's true that cases of food poisoning are not unknown. As well as couscous and pastilla, there are spicy **merguez sausages**, salads, fried fish and – for the more adventurous – **sheep's heads** complete with eyes.

To partake, sit on one of the benches and order. If you want a drink the stallholders will send a boy to get it for you. Note that stalls that don't clearly display their prices are likely to overcharge you mercilessly, so ask the price before ordering. If bread and olives are placed in front of you, you will be charged for them. You can avoid all this by just having a bowl of **harira** at one of the soup stalls.

Besides sit-down meals, you'll find exotic snacks on offer too. Over towards the eastern side of the square, a group of stalls offer a food much loved in Morocco – **stewed snails**. The stallholder ladles servings out of a simmering vat, and you eat the snails with a pin or toothpick before slurping back the soup they are stewed in. Just south of the main food stalls are a row of vendors selling **khoudenjal**, a hot, spicy infusion based on dried galangal and said to be an aphrodisiac. It's usually accompanied by a spicy confection made of flour and ground nuts, and served by the spoonful.

THE JEMAA EL FNA AND THE KOUTOUBIA

Kassabine Café

MAP p.28, POCKET MAP B11
77 Rue Dabbachi, by Kissariat Quessabine
ⓘ 0665 293796. Daily 8am–midnight.

The sunny terrace of this bright little café-restaurant has a perfect vista over the busy street below and views all the way down the western branch of the Jemaa el Fna. The tajines are lovingly made and include a wonderful beef with courgettes as well as old favourites like beef with prunes and almonds or chicken with lemon and olive, all for around 50dh.

Le Marrakchi

MAP p.28, POCKET MAP B12
52 Rue des Banques ⓘ 0524 443377,
ⓦ lemarrakchi.com. Daily noon–midnight.

High up above the square, *Le Marrakchi* has imperial but intimate decor and impeccable service. The food, too, is superb, and includes delicious pastilla, and several couscous and tajine options, including vegetarian versions. Main dishes are mostly around 130–180dh. Licensed.

Le Tobsil

MAP p.28, POCKET MAP A12
22 Derb Moulay Abdallah Ben Hezzaien

Le Tobsil

ⓘ 0524 444052. Mon & Wed–Sun 7.30–11pm.

The Moroccan cuisine is sumptuous at this intimate riad, which is considered by many to be the finest restaurant in town. It's reached by heading south down a little alley just east of Bab Laksour. Highlights include a delicious pastilla and the most aromatic couscous you could imagine, though the wine (included in the price) doesn't match the food in quality. The set menu – which changes daily – is 640dh. Worth booking ahead.

Tajine and Tanjia

Morocco's most typical dish is the **tajine**, a term that correctly refers not to the food itself – vegetables piled up around a meat core – but rather to the vessel in which it is cooked, a heavy ceramic plate crowned with a conical ceramic lid in which the contents are cooked slowly over a low heat, or over charcoal. The two classic tajines are chicken with olives and pickled lemon, and beef or lamb with prunes and almonds.

More specific to Marrakesh is the **tanjia** (also spelt tangia or tanzhiya), a jug in which beef or lamb are stewed even more slowly. The traditional way to cook a tanjia is in the embers of a bathhouse furnace, and indeed if you order in advance at diners such as *Hadj Mustapha* (see p.32), the meat and seasonings (garlic, cumin, nutmeg and other spices) will be placed in the urn for you and taken to the man who stokes the furnace at the local hammam. When the urn emerges from the embers a few hours later, the meat is tender and ready to eat.

Les Prémices

MAP p.28, POCKET MAP B12
Pl Jemaa el Fna ☏ 0524 391970.
Daily 8.30am–midnight.

Les Prémices serves decent
Moroccan and European food,
including tasty gazpacho, good-
value tajines, fish, pizzas and even
crème brûlée. It's on the very
southeastern corner of the square,
but close enough for a view of
the action, and very moderately
priced (you can eat well for 120dh,
very well for 160dh).

Pizzeria Portofino

MAP p.28, POCKET MAP A12
279 Av Mohammed V ☏ 0524 391665.
Daily noon–midnight.

The wood-oven pizzas (55–70dh)
here are well cooked, if slightly
bland, and the ambience is quite
posh, with white tablecloths and
uniformed waiters. They also
have pasta (70–120dh) and a
"Marrakshi" lamb risotto (80dh).

Restaurant Argana

MAP p.28, POCKET MAP B12
North side of Pl Jemaa el Fna ☏ 0524
445350. Daily 8am–midnight.

Closed for some years following
an infamous 2011 bomb attack,
the *Argana* is open again and
has the best vantage point over
the action in the square. There's
a posh café on the ground floor
and a good (but not expensive)
restaurant upstairs, where a tasty
tajine will set you back all of
40–100dh.

Restaurant Oscar Progrès

MAP p.28, POCKET MAP B13
20 Rue Bani Marine ☏ 0666 937147.
Daily noon–11pm.

One of the best budget restaurants
in town, with friendly service
and large servings of couscous
(go for that or the brochettes in
preference to the tajines, which are
rather bland). You can fill up here
for around 70dh, or be a real pig
and choose the 120dh set menu.

Les Prémices

Taj'in Darna

MAP p.28, POCKET MAP B12
50 Pl Jemaa el Fna ☏ 0661 311310,
🌐 tajindarna.com. Daily 7am–11pm.

In this great location on the
northeastern arm of the Jemaa,
you can dine on a variety of tajines,
from chicken with lemon and olive
(40dh) to the less familiar lamb
with figs and walnuts (75dh) or
rfisa (chicken with onions, lentils
and *msimmen*; 70dh).

Bar

Grand Hotel Tazi

MAP p.28, POCKET MAP B13
Corner Rue Bab Agnaou and Rue el
Mouahidine ☏ 0524 442787. Daily 6am–
midnight.

This was once the only place in
the Medina where you could get
a drink, and it's still the cheapest
(beers from 30dh). There's nothing
fancy about the bar – squeezed
in between the restaurant and the
lobby – but it manages to be neither
rough nor pretentious, a rare feat
among Marrakesh drinking dens.

The Northern Medina

Just north of the Jemaa el Fna begins the bustling main souk – or market – area, which is focused on a central thoroughfare, Souk Smarine, and is great for souvenir shopping. Originally, each souk was clearly defined, with one street selling this and another selling that, though these distinctions have now blurred somewhat. Among the most interesting souks are the Rahba Kedima, with its quirky apothecary stalls, and the dyers' souk, hung with brightly coloured hanks of freshly dyed wool. North of the souks are the small but architecturally important Almoravid Koubba, the Marrakesh Museum and the beautifully decorated Ben Youssef Medersa. Beyond, in all directions, stretches a vast residential area with more workaday shops and few tourists. The area is not devoid of attractions, however, containing a couple of important religious shrines and the city's stinky but fascinating tanneries.

Souk Smarine

MAP p.38, POCKET MAP B11
Busy and crowded, Souk Smarine, the souks' main thoroughfare, is covered along its whole course by an iron

Souk Smarine

trellis with slats across it that restricts the sun to **shafts of light** dappling everything beneath, especially in the early afternoon. Historically the street was dominated by the sale of textiles and clothing. Today, classier tourist "bazaars" are moving in, with American Express signs in the windows, but there are still dozens of shops in the arcades selling and tailoring traditional shirts and kaftans.

Other shops specialize in multicoloured cotton skullcaps and in **fezzes** (*tarbouche fassi* in Arabic), which originate from the city of Fez in northern Morocco. The feeling of being in a labyrinth of hidden treasures is heightened by the **passages** in between the shops, many of which lead through to small covered markets. The occasional stucco-covered doorways between shops are entrances to mosques – havens of spiritual refreshment amid the bustle.

Rahba Kedima

MAP p.38, POCKET MAP B11–C11

Souk Smarine narrows just before the fork at its northern end. The passageways to the right (east) here lead through to Rahba Kedima, an open marketplace with stalls in the middle and around the outside.

Immediately to the right as you go in is **Souk Loghzal**, once a market for slaves, more recently for wool, but now mainly selling secondhand clothes. In Rahba Kedima itself, the most interesting stalls are those belonging to the **apothecaries** in the southwest corner of the square, selling **traditional cosmetics** – earthenware saucers of cochineal (*kashiniah*) for lip-rouge, powdered kohl eyeliner (usually lead sulphide, which is toxic), henna (the only cosmetic unmarried Moroccan women are supposed to use) and sticks of *suek* (walnut root or bark) for cleaning teeth. The same stalls also sell herbal and animal ingredients still in widespread use for spells and medicinal cures. As well as aphrodisiac roots and tablets, you'll see dried pieces of lizard and stork, fragments of beaks, talons and other bizarre animal products. Some shops (to be avoided) also sell gazelle skulls, leopard skins and other products from illegally poached endangered wild animals. The *Café des Épices* (see p.48) overlooks the square and is a good place to take a breather.

La Criée Berbère

MAP p.38, POCKET MAP C11
Souk des Tapis.

Until the French occupied the city in 1912, La Criée Berbère (the Berber auction) was the site of **slave auctions**, held just before sunset every Wednesday, Thursday and Friday. Most of the slaves had been kidnapped and marched here with the camel caravans from

Rahba Kedima

West Africa – those too weak to make it were left to die en route. Happily, only rugs and carpets are sold here nowadays.

Kissaria

MAP p.38, POCKET MAP B10

A covered market at the heart of the souks, the Kissaria was originally set up as the souk for rich imported **fabrics**. It remains the centre for cloth and clothing, with an array of beautiful dresses, flowing headscarves and roll upon roll of fine material on show.

Souk Sabbaghine

MAP p.38, POCKET MAP B10

The Souk Sabbaghine (or Souk des Teinturiers, the **dyers' souk**) is west of the Kissaria and very near the sixteenth-century Mouassine Mosque and fountain. On a good day, it has a splendid array of freshly dyed sheaves of wool in a multitude of colours hung out to dry. At other times you'll barely see any at all, though you can still take a look as the dyers boil up their tints and prepare the wool for treatment.

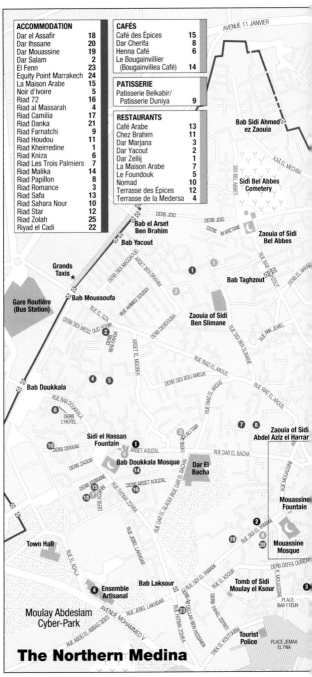

ACCOMMODATION

Dar el Assafir	18
Dar Ihssane	20
Dar Mouassine	19
Dar Salam	2
El Fenn	23
Equity Point Marrakech	24
La Maison Arabe	15
Noir d'Ivoire	5
Riad 72	16
Riad al Massarah	4
Riad Camilia	17
Riad Danka	21
Riad Farnatchi	9
Riad Houdou	11
Riad Kheirredine	1
Riad Kniza	6
Riad Les Trois Palmiers	7
Riad Malika	14
Riad Papillon	8
Riad Romance	3
Riad Safa	13
Riad Sahara Nour	10
Riad Star	12
Riad Zolah	25
Riyad el Cadi	22

CAFÉS

Café des Épices	15
Dar Cherifa	8
Henna Café	6
Le Bougainvillier	
(Bougainvillea Café)	14

PATISSERIE

Patisserie Belkabir/	
Patisserie Duniya	9

RESTAURANTS

Café Arabe	13
Chez Brahim	11
Dar Marjana	3
Dar Yacout	2
Dar Zellij	1
La Maison Arabe	7
Le Foundouk	5
Nomad	10
Terrasse des Épices	12
Terrasse de la Medersa	4

AVENUE 11 JANVIER

Bab Sidi Ahmed
ez Zaouia

KAÂ EL MECHRA

Sidi Bel Abbes
Cemetery

Zaouia of Sidi
Bel Abbes

DERB JDID

DERB M'ARETANE

Bab el Arset
Ben Brahim

Bab Yacout

Bab Taghzout

Grands
Taxis

Bab Moussoufa

Gare Routière
(Bus Station)

Zaouia of Sidi
Ben Slimane

RUE EL GZA

RUE AHMED SOUSSI

ARSET BEN BRAHIM

DERB SIDI MASSAOUD

DERB DERDOUBA

DERB SIDI MESS OUD SIHIR

DERB BEN FAYDA

ARSET EL MSIBER

RUE RIAD EL AROUS

RUE SIDI BEN SLIMANE

Bab Doukkala

RUE BAB DOUKKALA

DERB L'HOTEL

DERB SIDI BOU AMEUR

RUE RIAD EL AROUS

Sidi el Hassan
Fountain

RUE ARSET AOUZAL

DERB DEKKAK

DERB SIDI AL TAYR

Zaouia of Sidi
Abdel Aziz el Harrar

Bab Doukkala Mosque

DERB ZAOUIA

RUE DAR EL BACHA

Dar El
Bacha

DERB FERRIANE

RUE FATIMA ZOHRA

DERB ASSET AOUZAL

DERB BISSARA

RUE DAR EL GLAOUI

RUE DAR EL BACHA

Mouassine
Fountain

RUE MOUASSINE

Town Hall

RUE JEBEL LAKHDAR

RUE EL JDID

RUE SIDI EL YAMANI

Mouassine
Mosque

DERB DEFFA OURBA

RUE MOUASSINE

Moulay Abdeslam
Cyber-Park

Ensemble
Artisanal

Bab Laksour

Tomb of Sidi
Moulay el Ksour

PLACE
BAB FTEUH

RUE EL KSOUR

RUE SIDI EL YAMANI

RUE FAHL ZEFRITI

AVENUE MOHAMMED V

RUE JEBEL LAKHDAR

RUE FATIMA ZOHRA

RUE DELLAH BEN HASSIAN

DERB FAHL ZEFRITI

TREK EL YOUTOUBIA

Tourist
Police

PLACE JEMAA
EL FNA

RUE ABOU EL ABBAS SBITI

The Northern Medina

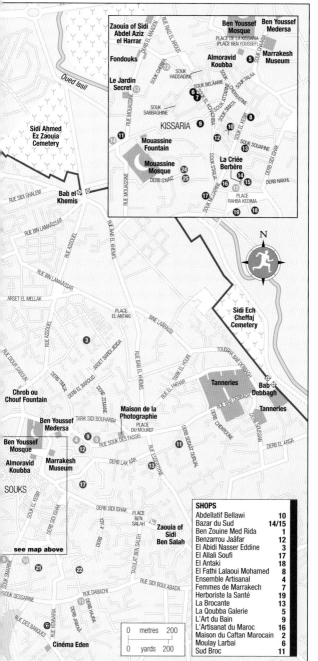

Zaouia of Sidi Abdel Aziz el Harrar

Fondouks

Le Jardin Secret **13**

Ben Youssef Mosque

Ben Youssef Medersa

Almoravid Koubba **5**

Marrakesh Museum

SOUK HADDADINE

SOUK BELAARIE **6**
7

RUE BAB EL AROUSS

DERB EL MAEDEN

RUE OULD EL AROUS

SOUK CHERIFIA

SOUK ATTARINE

SOUK CHRATINE

SOUK TALAA

SOUK SMATA

PLACE DE LA KISSARIA
(PLACE BEN YOUSSEF)

SOUK SABBAGHINE

SOUK EL KEBIR **8**

10

SOUK SOUAFINE

9

KISSARIA

11
14

Mouassine Fountain

12

13

La Criée Berbère

SOUK STIAA

SOUK LARBA

SOUK LAKHMIYA

14
15

DERB SIDI ISHAK

DERB NAKHIL

Mouassine Mosque **24**
25

DERB G.NAIZ

16

17

PLACE RAHBA KEDIMA

19
18

Oued Issil

Sidi Ahmed Ez Zaouia Cemetery

Bab el Khemis

RUE MOUASSINE

RUE SIDI GHALEM

RUE BIN LAMAASSAR

RUE BIN LAMAASSAR

RUE EL KSSOUR

ARSET EL MELLAK

RUE BAB EL KHEMIS

RUE RIAD EL MAEDEN

RUE INOUS SABOUN

PLACE EL ANTAKI

BINE LAARASSI

ARSET BARDI WIDDA

RUE BAB EL KHEMIS

DERB TRAKA

DERB EL BAROUD

DERB ZEMANE

TARIK EL MOURI

TARIK EL FAKHAR

Sidi Ech Cheffaj Cemetery

TOUDGH BAB DEBBAGH

3

Chrob ou Chouf Fountain

Ben Youssef Medersa

Ben Youssef Mosque

Almoravid Koubba

Marrakesh Museum

SOUKS

TARIK SIDI BOUHARBA

4 **9**

12

DERB LAK AAR

17

RUE SOUK DES FASSIS

Maison de la Photographie

PLACE DU MOUKEF

RUE ESSATINE

11

13

DERB SEBAAT OUBDAL

RUE EL MOUKEF

DERB BAB DEBBAGH

Tanneries

Bab Debbagh

Tanneries

DERB CHERKOUNE

DERB SOUSSAN

DERB EL ARSA

see map above

SOUK EL KEBIR

DERB SIDI ISHAK

PLACE BEN SALAH

DERB K.KAD

DERB SIDI ISHAK

TAOULAT BEN SALAH

Zaouia of Sidi Ben Salah

RUE SIDI BOULABADA

10

21

22

SOUK SMARINE

SOUK GESSARINE

RUE DES BANQUES

RUE KENNARIA

RUE DABACHI

DERB DABACHI

DERB JAMAA

@

Cinéma Eden

N

| 0 | metres | 200 |
| 0 | yards | 200 |

SHOPS

Abdellatif Bellawi	10
Bazar du Sud	14/15
Ben Zouine Med Rida	1
Benzarrou Jaâfar	12
El Abidi Nasser Eddine	3
El Allali Soufi	17
El Antaki	18
El Fathi Lalaoui Mohamed	8
Ensemble Artisanal	4
Femmes de Marrakech	7
Herboriste la Santé	19
La Brocante	13
La Qoubba Galerie	5
L'Art du Bain	9
L'Artisanat du Maroc	16
Maison du Caftan Marocain	2
Moulay Larbai	6
Sud Broc	11

Souk Haddadine and Souk Cherratine

MAP p.38, POCKET MAP B10 & C10

It's easy to locate Souk Haddadine, the **ironmongers' souk**, by ear – just head towards the source of the bangings and clangings as the artisans shape raw metal into decorative window grilles, lampstands and furniture. Close at hand you'll find Souk Cherratine, the **leatherworkers' souk**, full of workshops where hats, slippers and other goods are cut and stitched by hand. There are also specialist shops whose sole occupation is to grind and sharpen tools.

Marrakesh Museum

MAP p.38, POCKET MAP C10

Pl de la Kissaria (Pl Ben Youssef) ☎ 0524 441893, ⊕ www.museedemarrakech.ma. Daily 9am–6pm. 50dh.

This magnificent late nineteenth-century palace, originally built for Morocco's defence minister, is now a museum housing exhibitions of Moroccan **art and sculpture**. It's the building itself, however, that's most memorable, especially the warren of rooms that was once the

Almoravid Koubba

hammam, and the now-covered **inner courtyard** with its huge brass lamp hung above a central fountain.

Almoravid Koubba

MAP p.38, POCKET MAP C10

South side of Pl de la Kissaria (Pl Ben Youssef). Daily 9am–6pm, but closed for restoration at time of writing.

Situated well below the current ground level, the Almoravid Koubba (correctly called the Koubba Ba'adyin) doesn't look like much, but this small, two-storey structure is the only building in Morocco to survive intact from the eleventh-century Almoravid dynasty, whose style lies at the root of all Moroccan architecture. The windows on each side exhibit the classic shapes of Moroccan design – as do the merlons (the Christmas-tree-like battlements). Its motifs – notably pine cones, palms and acanthus leaves – appear again in later buildings such as the nearby Ben Youssef Medersa. The Almoravid Koubba was probably an ablutions annexe to the **Ben Youssef Mosque** opposite, which, like almost all the Almoravids' buildings, was demolished and rebuilt by the succeeding Almohad dynasty. The *koubba* is currently closed, supposedly for restoration, but can be seen very well from Place de la Kissaria.

Ben Youssef Medersa

MAP p.38, POCKET MAP C10

Off Pl de la Kissaria (Pl Ben Youssef). Daily 9am–6pm. 20dh.

Just north of the Marrakesh Museum, and attached to the Ben Youssef Mosque, is the Ben Youssef Medersa, a **religious school** where students learned the Koran by rote. The medersa was founded in the fourteenth century and almost completely rebuilt in the 1560s under the Saadian dynasty. The central courtyard, its carved **cedar lintels**

Ben Youssef Medersa

weathered almost flat on the most exposed side, is unusually large. Along two sides run wide, sturdy, columned arcades, and above them are some of the windows of the dormitory quarters, which are reached by stairs from the entry vestibule. The decoration is at its best preserved and most elaborate in the **prayer hall**, at the far end of the main court. Notable here, as in the courtyard's cedar carving, is a predominance of pine cone and palm motifs, especially around the horseshoe-arched mihrab. The inscriptions are quotations from the Koran, the most common being its opening invocation: "In the name of God, the Compassionate, the Merciful".

Fondouks

One of the most characteristic types of building in the Medina is the **fondouk** or *caravanserai*, originally inns used by visiting merchants when they were in Marrakesh to trade in its souks. *Fondouks* have a courtyard in the middle surrounded by what were originally stables, while the upper level contained rooms for the merchants. Some *fondouks* date back to Saadian times (1520–1669).

Today, Marrakesh's *fondouks* are in varying states of repair; some have become private residences, others commercial premises. Some have been converted to house tourist souvenir shops, and welcome visitors, but even in others, the doors to the courtyards are often left open, and no one seems to mind if you have a look.

Interesting *fondouks* include: a group on Rue Dar el Bacha by the junction with Rue Mouassine, several of which welcome visitors; a couple just south of the junction on Rue Mouassine itself; a row on the south side of Rue Souk des Fassis, behind the Ben Youssef Medersa; a few on Rue Amesfah, north of the Ben Youssef Mosque; and one directly opposite the Chrob ou Chouf fountain. And of course there's **Le Foundouk** (see p.50) and **Terrasse le Medersa** (see p.51), where you can eat in a converted *fondouk*.

Chrob ou Chouf Fountain

Chrob ou Chouf Fountain

MAP p.38, POCKET MAP G4
220 Rue Assouel, a little way north of
Pl de la Kissaria (Pl Ben Youssef).

This small sixteenth-century
recessed fountain (its name means
"drink and admire") is mainly
notable for its carved cedar lintel,
which incorporates calligraphy
and stalactite-like projections.
Back in the days before people had
running water at home, paying to
put up a fountain was a pious act
of charity. Religious institutions
and wealthy philanthropists had
them installed to provide not only
drinking water, but also a place to
wash – in particular to perform
the ritual ablutions demanded by
the Koran before prayer.

Zaouia of Sidi Abdel Aziz el Harrar

MAP p.38, POCKET MAP B10
Rue Mouassine.

Sidi Abdel Aziz el Harrar (d.1508)
was an Islamic scholar who –
unusually among Marrakesh's
Seven Saints (see box below) –
was actually born in Marrakesh,
though he made his name in Fez.
His *zaouia* is one of the smallest of
the Seven Saints' shrines.

Le Jardin Secret

MAP p.38, POCKET MAP B10
121 Rue Mouassine ℡ 0524 390040,
Ⓦ lejardinsecretmarrakech.com. Daily: Feb
& March 9.30am–6.30pm; April–Sept
9.30am–7.30pm; Oct–Jan 9.30am–5.30pm.
50dh; tower 30dh extra.

This beautifully restored garden of
an old Medina mansion describes
itself as an "open-air museum",
to show what medieval gardens
were like, most importantly, their
irrigation system. You can climb

The Seven Saints of Marrakesh

Some two hundred holy men and women, known as **marabouts**,
are buried in Marrakesh. A *marabout*'s tomb can become the
centrepiece of a mosque-mausoleum called a **zaouia**, often the
focus for a brotherhood of the *marabout*'s followers, who usually
belong to the mystic branch of Islam known as **Sufism**. It's widely
believed that praying to God at the tomb of a *marabout* attracts a
special *beraka* (blessing).

Marrakesh's seven most prominent *marabouts* are usually
referred to in English as the "**Seven Saints**" of the city, though they
have little in common aside from being buried here. The most
prominent, Sidi Bel Abbes, is pretty much the city's patron saint.

Though non-Muslims are not allowed to enter the tombs, you
can certainly see them all from the outside, and a couple – **Sidi Bel
Abbes** (see p.44) and **Sidi Abdel Aziz el Harrar** (see above) – are
definitely worth a look.

the tower and get a rooftop view. The high prices keep out the hoi-polloi, which makes it a peaceful retreat.

Bab Doukkala Mosque

MAP p.38, POCKET MAP F4
Rue Bab Doukkala. Gallery daily
9.30am–1pm & 3.30–7.30pm. Free.

Serving the lively Bab Doukkala quarter, this *pisé* mosque with its elegant brick minaret was constructed in 1557–58 on the orders of Lalla Messaouda, mother of Ahmed el Mansour, the most illustrious sultan of the Saadian dynasty. On the main street in front of the mosque is the impressive three-bay **Sidi el Hassan fountain**, now converted into a small art gallery.

Zaouia of Sidi Ben Salah

MAP p.38, POCKET MAP H5
Pl Ben Salah.

This fourteenth-century holy man's tomb is one of the few important buildings in the Medina to have been put up under the Merenid dynasty, who had moved the Moroccan capital from Marrakesh to its rival city of Fez. The most prominent feature is the handsome **minaret**, covered with brilliant green tiles in a *darj w ktarf* pattern.

The Tanneries

MAP p.38, POCKET MAP J4
Along and off Rue Bab Debbagh.

Marrakesh's tanneries are sited at the edge of the city not only because of the smell, but also for access to water: a stream, the Oued Issil, runs just outside the walls. One tannery that's easy to find is Tannerie Attanjir on the north side of the street about 200m before Bab Debbagh, opposite the blue-tiled fountain, with another one about 200m further west. If you want to take a closer look at the **tanning process**, come in the morning, when the cooperatives are at work. There is no charge to visit – ignore hustlers who tell you otherwise.

Maison de la Photographie

MAP p.38, POCKET MAP H4
46 Rue Souk des Fassis ☎ 0524 385721,
ⓦ maisondelaphotographie.ma.
Daily 9.30am–7pm. 40dh.

The Maison de la Photographie houses a reasonably interesting collection of early twentieth-century (and a few late nineteenth-century) photographs of Morocco, some made from glass negatives. The photographs are exhibited over three floors, with one room dedicated to pictures of the Jemaa el Fna, and the terrace gives good views over the Medina rooftops.

The Tanneries

Bab Debbagh

MAP p.38, POCKET MAP J4

Among the more interesting of Marrakesh's city gates, Bab Debbagh is supposedly Almoravid in design. Over the years it must have been almost totally rebuilt, but its defensive purpose is still apparent: three internal **chicanes** are placed in such a manner as to force anyone attempting to storm it to make numerous turns. Just before the gate, several shops on the left give good **views** over the tanneries from their roofs. Shopkeepers may invite you up, but agree the price first or you'll be mercilessly overcharged.

Outside the gate, across Rue des Remparts, Oued Issil was once the city's main water source, but now far too polluted, and prone to flooding in heavy rain.

Bab el Khemis

MAP p.38, POCKET MAP H2

This beautiful gate, originally Almoravid though rebuilt under the Almohads, is surrounded by concentric rings of decoration and topped with Christmas-tree-like castellations. Its name, meaning "Thursday Gate", is a reference to the market held outside, 300m to the north. You'll find stalls out

most days, but the main market is on Thursday mornings, where everything from bric-a-brac and old furniture to local produce and retro clothing is for sale.

Zaouia of Sidi Bel Abbes

MAP p.38, POCKET MAP G3
Rue Bab Taghzout.

The most important of Marrakesh's Seven Saints (see box, p.42), twelfth-century **Sidi Bel Abbes** was a prolific performer of miracles, particularly famed for giving sight to the blind. The huge mosque that now houses his tomb, with a green-tiled roof and surrounding outbuildings, dates largely from an early eighteenth-century reconstruction. It lies just north of **Bab Taghzout**, which was one of the gates of the Medina until the eighteenth century, when Sultan Mohammed Abdallah extended the walls north to include the Sidi Bel Abbes quarter. As with all *zaouias*, non-Muslims are not allowed to enter the complex but may take a look in from the outside. The foundation that runs the *zaouia* also owns much of the surrounding quarter and is engaged in charitable work, distributing food each evening to the blind.

Bab el Khemis

Abdellatif Bellawi

Shops

Abdellatif Bellawi

MAP p.38, POCKET MAP B10
56 & 103 Kissariat Lossta, between Souk
el Kebir and Souk Attarine ☎ 0668 049114.
Mon–Thurs, Sat & Sun 9am–5pm.

This pair of costume-jewellery and knick-knack shops has a great selection of beads and bangles, including Berber bracelets from the Atlas in chunky solid silver, traditional Berber necklaces, West African money beads and necklaces from as far away as Yemen. There are more frivolous items too, like the cowrie-encrusted Gnaoua caps hanging outside the door, plus rings, earrings and woollen Berber belts.

Bazar du Sud

MAP p.38, POCKET MAP C11
14 & 117 Souk des Tapis ☎ 0524 443004.
Daily 9.30am–7pm.

There are carpets here from all over the south of Morocco. Most are claimed to be old (if you prefer them spanking new, pop next door to Bazar Jouti at nos. 16 & 119), and most are coloured with wonderful natural dyes such as saffron (yellow), cochineal (red) and indigo (blue). A large carpet could cost 5000dh or more, but you might be able to find a small rug for around 500dh.

Ben Zouine Med Rida

MAP p.38, POCKET MAP F4
142 Rue Arset Aouzal ☎ 0670 465761.
Mon–Thurs, Sat & Sun 9am–7pm,
Fri 8am–noon.

For a tailor-made, local-style shirt or blouse, be it in cotton, linen or wool, this is the place to come, though opening hours can be a bit haphazard (morning is the best time to catch them). You just choose your cloth, get measured up, specify what buttons or even embroidered design you want, and come back a day or two later to collect. Expect to pay around 500–1000dh.

Benzarrou Jaâfar

MAP p.38, POCKET MAP B11
1 Kissariat Drouj, off Souk Smata by
no. 116 ☎ 0524 443351. Daily 9am–9pm.

There are any number of shops in this souk selling Moroccan slippers, or babouches, but while emporiums in the Souk des Babouches specialize in new designs, this trio of shops in a little corner of the Kissaria is the best place to come for the traditional variety. Both men's and women's are available, in various colours. Prices are displayed and start at 50dh, and there's no pressure or hard sell.

El Abidi Nasser Eddine

MAP p.38, POCKET MAP B11
9 Souk Smarine ☎ 0524 441066.
Daily 9am–9pm.

A discreet and rather upmarket shop for antique jewellery, or modern designer pieces, all exquisite, all expensive, plus silverware, manuscripts and some very fine *objets d'art*. A place for those seeking something finer than the usual souk wares.

El Allali Soufi

MAP p.38, POCKET MAP B11
125 Souk Nejjarine, opposite the alley to
Pl Rahba Kedima ☎ 0668 440399. Daily
9am–8pm.

This little place sells silver – old
and new – whether in the form of
jewellery, old coins, spoons and
ladles, teapots, or just odd little
curiosities (some in other metals,
such as brass). Pricey, but worth
a browse.

El Antaki

MAP p.38, POCKET MAP C11
54 Souk Labtana, off Pl Rahba Kedima
☎ 0678 106499. Mon–Thurs, Sat & Sun
9am–7pm.

In what was once the sheepskin
souk, and is now the basket souk,
this shop has fixed, displayed
prices. Goods on offer include
baskets, coasters, tablemats and
boxes, made of palm fronds or
various reeds and rushes, from
10dh upwards.

El Fathi Lalaoui Mohamed

MAP p.38, POCKET MAP C10
8 Souk Serrajine, off Souk el Kebir ☎ 0668
964629. Mon–Thurs, Sat & Sun 9am–7pm.

This shop originally sold saddles
for horses (and the one next door
still does), but now specializes
in selling objects made from the

Ensemble Artisanal

layer of woollen felt that formed
part of the traditional saddle –
turned into bags, hats, even beads.
Each item is made in a single piece
with a big splash of colour. Bags
go for 150–250dh, hats for 100dh.

Ensemble Artisanal

MAP p.38, POCKET MAP E5
Av Mohammed V, midway between the
Koutoubia and Bab Nkob ☎ 0524 443503.
Mon–Sat 9am–7pm, Sun 9am–noon.

This government-run complex of
small arts and crafts shops holds a
reasonable range of goods, notably
leather, textiles and carpets. The
prices, which are more or less
fixed, are a good gauge of the
going rate if you intend to bargain
elsewhere. At the back are a dozen
or so workshops where you can
watch young people learning a
range of crafts.

Femmes de Marrakech

MAP p.38, POCKET MAP B10
67 Souk el Kchachbia, west of Almoravid
Koubba ☎ 0665 343472. Mon–Thurs, Sat &
Sun 10am–6pm (later in summer).

A dress shop run by a women's
cooperative, who create their
own garments and also sell – on
a fair-trade basis – clothes made
at home by other women. The
dresses are handmade from pure
cotton and linen fabrics in a mix
of Moroccan and Western styles,
with colours ranging from sober
pinks and greys to bright orange
tie-dye.

Herboriste la Santé

MAP p.38, POCKET MAP C11
152 Pl Rahba Kedima, on the south side of
the square ☎ 0666 310728. Daily
8am–9pm.

One of a row of apothecary shops
on the south and west side of
the Rahba Kedima, but unlike
some others, this one doesn't sell
dubious animal products. The
genial staff will patiently explain
the wondrous properties of the
various herbs, spices, scents and
traditional cosmetics they sell.

La Brocante

La Brocante

MAP p.38, POCKET MAP C11
16 Souk Souafine, off Souk el Kebir.
☎ 0650 221938. Tues–Sun 10am–1pm
& 3–6.30pm.

A little shop with all sorts of
antique curiosities: corkscrews,
toys, watches, medals, enamelled
metal signs and what would be
bric-a-brac, but for the fact that it's
been chosen with a tasteful eye.

La Qoubba Galerie

MAP p.38, POCKET MAP C10
91 Souk Talaa ☎ 0524 390371,
ⓦ qoubbagalerie.com. Daily 9am–6.30pm.

Paintings and sculptures by
contemporary Moroccan artists
are displayed in an attractive little
two-room gallery off Place de la
Kissaria (Pl Ben Youssef). The
gallery sells works by 62 artists, all
with very different styles.

La Qoubba Galerie

L'Art du Bain

MAP p.38, POCKET MAP B10
13 Souk el Labadine ☎ 0668 445942,
ⓦ lartdubainshop.com. Mon–Thurs, Sat &
Sun 10am–6pm, Fri 3–6pm.

This place sells a big range of
soaps made with one hundred-
percent Moroccan essential
oils, and exotic ingredients such
as musk, ambergris, ghassoul
(natural mud shampoo) and
camel's milk, all available in small
(25dh) or large (40dh).

L'Artisanat du Maroc

MAP p.38, POCKET MAP B11.
68 Souk Nejjarine, part of Souk el Kebir.
Mon, Tues, Thurs, Sat & Sun 10am–6pm,
Wed 11am–6pm, Fri 2–6pm.

A great little selection of wooden
kitchen implements, including
handmade spoons in all sizes,
from ladles for eating *harira* to
teaspoons, plus paddles for honey,
and pairs of wooden scissors (for
cutting fresh pasta, in case you
wondered). Prices for the small
items start at just 10dh.

Maison du Caftan Marocain

MAP p.38, POCKET MAP B11
65 Rue Sidi el Yamani ☎ 0524 441051.
Daily 10am–8.30pm.

All sorts of robes, tunics and
kaftans are available in this
wonderful shop, from see-through
glittery gowns and sequinned
tunics to embroidered silk kaftans
that make sumptuous housecoats
(albeit mostly at prices in excess of
2000dh). Most are for women, but
there are a few men's garments.
Past customers include Jean-Paul
Gaultier and Mick Jagger.

La Qoubba Galerie

Moulay Larbai

MAP p.38, POCKET MAP B10
96 Souk el Kchachbia ☏ 0671 374942.
Mon–Thurs, Sat & Sun 8am–7pm,
Fri 8am–noon & 5–7pm.

Moulay Larbai's claim to fame is that it was he who first started making mirrors framed with small pieces of mirror or of coloured glass. He still makes the best ones in the souk, with Iraqi-style stained glass for the colours, and they come in various shapes and sizes. Prices start at around 50dh.

Sud Broc

MAP p.38, POCKET MAP B11
65 Rue Mouassine ☏ 0666 075155.
Daily 9am–1pm & 3–7pm.

A bric-a-brac shop with quite high prices (bargain hard), but it does have an interesting selection, including old cameras, watches, lighters – Zippos and imitation Zippos, old and new – and other relics of the good old days.

Cafés

Café des Épices

MAP p.38, POCKET MAP C11
73 Pl Rahba Kedima ☏ 0524 391770,
🌐 cafedesepices.net. Daily 9am–11pm.

Café offering refuge from the hubbub and views over the Rahba Kedima from the upper floor and the roof terrace. Drinks include orange juice, mint tea, coffee in various permutations, including spiced with cinnamon, and there are also sandwiches (40–50dh) and salads (50–55dh).

Dar Cherifa

MAP p.38, POCKET MAP B11
8 Derb Charfa Lakbir, Mouassine
☏ 0524 426463, 🌐 darcherifa.com.
Daily 10am–8pm (ring for entry).

For those who like a bit of culture with their tea and pastry, riad rental firm Marrakech Riads (see box, p.97) run an art-house literary café at their HQ. It's a

Dar Cherifa

lovely fifteenth-century riad, complete with antique doors, stucco and carved cedar, where you can stop for a spot of tea, a light lunch or even couscous (the best in the Medina, so they reckon). As well as food and refreshment, the café offers art exhibitions, cultural evenings, poetry readings (in Arabic, Berber and French) and even concerts.

Henna Café

MAP p.38, POCKET MAP F4
93 Rue Arset Aouzal ☏ 0656 566374,
🌐 hennacafemarrakech.com. Daily
noon–8pm.

As well as tea and coffee, this café offers salads and snacks that are slightly different from the Marrakesh norm (falafel in bread with salad, for example, at 40dh), and there's a roof terrace as well. They also have a henna menu, where you can choose a tattoo (50–550dh), and profits are ploughed into the local community.

Le Bougainvillier
(Bougainvillea café)

MAP p.38, POCKET MAP B11
33 Rue Mouassine ☏ 0524 378067. Daily
10am–10pm.

An upmarket café and quiet retreat in the middle of the Medina: handy for a break after a hard morning's shopping in the souks. Set in a secluded patio, it tries hard to be stylish, and generally succeeds, the lack of actual bougainvillea flowers being made up for by bougainvillea-pink paintwork and chairs. There are salads, sandwiches, cakes, juices, coffee and tea, but most of all it's a pleasant space in which to relax.

Patisserie

Patisserie Belkabir and Patisserie Duniya

MAP p.38, POCKET MAP B11
63–65 Souk Smarine, by the corner of Traverse el Ksour. Daily 10am–9pm.
Side by side, these shops specialize in traditional Moroccan sweetmeats, stuffed with nuts and drenched in syrup, which are particularly popular during the holy month of Ramadan (when of course they are eaten by night). A mixture (*mélange*) is 100dh a kilo – this price is posted up, but beware of them trying to charge a higher rate.

Restaurants

Café Arabe

MAP p.38, POCKET MAP B10
184 Rue Mouassine ☎ 0524 429728. Daily 10am–midnight (food served noon–11pm).
A sophisticated bar and restaurant in the heart of the Medina and very handy for the souks. As well as excellent Moroccan and European cooking, not to mention snappy service, there's a fine selection of alcoholic drinks including wines and cocktails, plus juices, teas and mocktails, served on the terrace, in the patio or in the salon. Expect to pay around 350dh plus drinks.

Dar Marjana

Chez Brahim

MAP p.38, POCKET MAP C11 & C12
38 Rue Dabbachi ☎ 0524 024709. Daily noon–11pm.
This budget restaurant, just a short walk from the Jemaa el Fna, offers rooftop dining with the usual range of Moroccan staples (salads, brochettes, tajines, couscous), and good-value set menus (60–120dh), the cheapest of which changes daily.

Dar Marjana

MAP p.38, POCKET MAP A10
15 Derb Sidi Ali Tair, off Rue Arset Aouzal ☎ 0524 385110, ⓦ darmarjanamarrakech .com. Mon & Wed–Sun from 8pm. Advance booking only.
This restaurant is housed in a beautiful early nineteenth-century palace. Look for the sign above the entrance to a passageway diagonally across the street from the corner of the Dar el Glaoui; take the passage and look for the green door facing you before a right turn. Among the tasty dishes they serve, two classics stand out: poultry pastilla and *couscous aux sept légumes*. The set menus cost 500–700dh including wine.

Dar Yacout

Dar Yacout

MAP p.38, POCKET MAP F3
79 Derb Sidi Ahmed Soussi ☎ 0524
382929, Ⓦ daryacout.com. Tues–Sun 8pm–
midnight.

Housed in a gorgeous old palace, the *Yacout* opened as a restaurant in 1987, its columns and fireplaces made over in super-smooth orange- and blue-striped *tadelakt* plaster, courtesy of American interior designer and Marrakesh resident Bill Willis. The owner was formerly Marrakesh's British consul. After a drink on the roof terrace, you move down into one of the intimate salons surrounding the courtyard for a selection of salads, followed by a tajine, then lamb couscous and dessert (the menu costs 700dh per person including wine). The classic Moroccan tajine of chicken with lemon and olives is a favourite here, but the fish version is also highly rated. The cuisine has in the past received Michelin plaudits, though standards are beginning to slip as the tour groups move in. Booking ahead is advised. The easiest way to get there is by *petit taxi* – the driver will usually walk you to the door.

Dar Zellij

MAP p.38, POCKET MAP F3
1 Kaa Essour, Sidi Ben Slimane ☎ 0524
382627, Ⓦ darzellij.com. Mon & Wed–Sun
7pm–midnight, plus Fri & Sat noon–3pm
& Sun 10am–3pm.

A seventeenth-century riad where you can take dinner on the patio or in one of the lounges, all decked out in red and super-comfortable. Start with Moroccan salad and *briouats* (filo pastry parcels – the Moroccan equivalent of a spring roll), followed by pastilla and then a tajine (vegetarian options are available), and round it off with sweet pastilla or orange in cinnamon. There's a choice of set menus at 300–750dh, plus lunch (Fri–Sun) at 200–250dh, not including drinks. Also, there's Sunday brunch at 180dh. Licensed.

La Maison Arabe

MAP p.38, POCKET MAP E4
1 Derb Assehbi, Rue Bab Doukkala
☎ 0524 387010, Ⓦ lamaisonarabe.com.
Daily noon–3pm & 7–11pm.

As well as being the city's best hotel (see p.100), *La Maison Arabe* is also one of its top eating places, with two restaurants, of which the Moroccan one serves up a 1200dh tasting menu for two including seasonal tajines and pastilla (or a veggie pastilla and veggie tajine for non-carnivores). The *Trois Saveurs* restaurant offers Moroccan, European and Asian dishes at around 120–250dh a go. Licensed.

Le Foundouk

MAP p.38, POCKET MAP C10
55 Rue Souk des Fassis ☎ 0524 378190,
Ⓦ foundouk.com. Mon, Tues & Thurs–Sun
7pm–midnight.

Housed in a beautifully converted former *fondouk*, this restaurant is conveniently located on the way from Ben Youssef Medersa to the tanneries. The menu has both Moroccan and international dishes, including tajines, *briouats*

Nomad

as *Café des Épices* (see p.48). It's well designed, with separate bays for each table giving diners their own space and a bit of privacy – handy if you want to use the free wi-fi – while still allowing you to enjoy the great views. Food is good and very moderately priced, with main dishes in the 90–180dh range. There's pastilla or a trio of Moroccan salads to start, and perhaps monkfish tajine to follow and crème brûlée and chocolate fondant for dessert.

Terrasse le Medersa

MAP p.38, POCKET MAP C10
Fondouk Lahbabi, 4 Rue de Souk des Fassis ☎ 0524 390719. Daily 10am–10pm.

On the terrace of a *fondouk* adjoining the roof of the Ben Youssef Medersa (hence its name), this unassuming little café-restaurant offers a variety of mocktails (35–40dh), juices and inexpensive Moroccan dishes (chicken tajine with lemon and olive, for example, at 55dh), served with a smile. On the downside, the seats could be larger and more comfortable.

and brochettes, as well as more adventurous dishes such as steak with mashed jerusalem artichokes and truffle oil, or duck with caramelized carrots. Main dishes go for 100–200dh. Licensed.

Nomad

MAP p.38, POCKET MAP B11
1 Derb Aarjane (off Pl Rahba Kedima)
☎ 0524 381609, ⓦ nomadmarrakech.com.
Daily noon–10.30pm.

This hip little restaurant offers a modern take on Moroccan cuisine, with light, fresh versions of classic dishes (mains 90–120dh), fish brought in daily from the coast, lots of vegetarian options (including vegetable pastilla), a mezze selection, and their own angle on dishes such as Tunisian *brick à l'oeuf* (egg in filo pastry) and a Moroccan-style hamburger. The terrace has great views over Place Rahba Kedima.

Terrasse des Épices

MAP p.38, POCKET MAP B10
15 Souk Cherifa ☎ 0524 375904,
ⓦ terrassedesepices.com.
Daily 11am–11pm.

This terrace restaurant, above the souks, is run by the same people

Terrasse des Épices

The Southern Medina and Agdal Gardens

The southern part of the Medina is less crowded and frenetic than the northern part, and is broken up into more distinct quarters. Its biggest attractions are the fabulous ruin of the El Badi Palace and the exquisite Saadian Tombs. Both lie within the Kasbah district, which was originally Marrakesh's walled citadel. To the east of here, and occupying a substantial area, is the Royal Palace, used by the king when visiting the city (and not open to the public). The area further east of this is the Mellah, once Morocco's largest Jewish ghetto; the extensive Agdal Gardens lie to the south. Between the Royal Palace and the Jemaa el Fna, the residential Riad Zitoun el Kedim and Riad Zitoun el Jedid quarters are home to two interesting museums and the beautiful Bahia Palace.

Dar Si Said

MAP p.54, POCKET MAP C13
Derb Si Said, off Rue Riad Zitoun el Jedid.
Daily except Tues 9am–4.45pm. 10dh.

A pleasing building, with beautiful pooled courtyards, scented with

Dar Si Said

lemons, palms and flowers, the Dar Si Said was built in the late nineteenth century as a palace for the brother of Bou Ahmed (see opposite) who, like Bou Ahmed himself, became royal chamberlain. It houses the impressive **Museum of Moroccan Arts**, which is particularly strong on eighteenth- and nineteenth-century woodwork, including furniture, Berber doors and window frames, and wonderful painted ceilings. There are also (upstairs) a number of traditional wedding **palanquins**, and an early eleventh-century **marble basin** from the Andalusian capital Córdoba, decorated with what seem to be heraldic eagles and griffins. Not all of these will necessarily be on show at any one time.

Maison Tiskiwin

MAP p.54, POCKET MAP C13
Derb el Bahia, off Rue Riad Zitoun el Jedid.
Daily 9am–12.30pm & 2.30–6pm. 20dh.

The Maison Tiskiwin houses a collection of Moroccan and Saharan artefacts from the

collection of Dutch anthropologist Bert Flint, which illustrate the cultural links across the desert resulting from the **caravan trade** between Morocco and Mali. Each room features carpets, fabrics, clothes and jewellery from a different region of the Sahara, with translations in English.

The Bahia Palace

MAP p.54, POCKET MAP H6
Rue Riad Zitoun el Jedid. Daily
9am–4.30pm. 10dh.

The Bahia Palace – its name means "brilliance" – was originally built in 1866–67 for the then grand vizier (akin to a prime minister), **Si Moussa**. In the 1890s it was extended by his son, **Bou Ahmed**, himself a grand vizier and regent to the sultan, who ascended the throne aged 14. There is a certain pathos to the empty, echoing chambers of the palace, and the inevitable passing of Bou Ahmed's influence and glory. When he died, the palace was looted by its staff, and his family driven out to starvation and ruin.

You enter the palace from the west, through an arcaded courtyard. This leads to a small riad (enclosed garden), part of Bou Ahmed's extension and decorated with beautiful carved stucco and cedarwood surrounds. The adjoining eastern salon leads through to the **great courtyard** of Si Moussa's palace, with a fountain in its centre and vestibules on all sides, each boasting a marvellous painted wooden ceiling.

South of the great courtyard is the large riad, the heart of Si Moussa's palace, fragrant with fruit trees and melodious with birdsong, approaching the very ideal of beauty in Arabic domestic architecture. The halls to the east and west are decorated with fine zellij fireplaces and painted wooden ceilings. You leave the palace via the private apartment built for Ahmed's wife, **Lalla Zinab**, where again it's worth looking up to check out the painted ceiling, carved stucco and stained-glass windows.

Place des Ferblantiers

MAP p.54, POCKET MAP H7
This tinsmiths' square, once part of a souk belonging to the Mellah (see p.56), is now dominated by the workshops of **lantern-makers** (see p.60). The Mellah's souk can be found through a doorway in the northeast corner of the square.

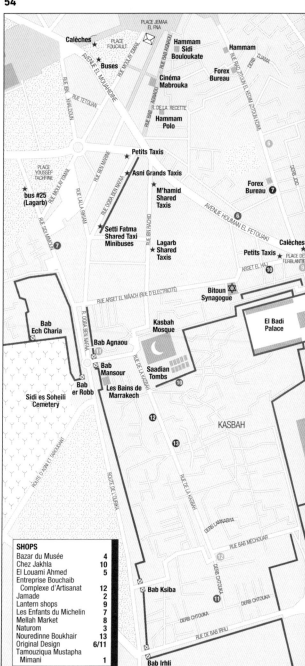

PLACE JEMAA EL FNA

★ Calèches
PLACE FOUCAULT

★ Buses

AVENUE EL MOUAHIDINE

RUE MOULAY ISMAIL

RUE IBN KHALDOUI

RUE TETOUAN

RUE BAB AGNAOU

RUE MOULAY ISMAIL

Hammam Sidi Bouloukate

RUE BAB AGNAOU

RUE RIAD ZITOUN EL KEDIM ZITOUN KDIM

Hammam

DERB DJAMA

Cinéma Mabrouka

Forex Bureau

R. DE LA RECETTE

Hammam Polo

6

PLACE YOUSSEF TACHFINE

★ bus #25 (Lagarb)

RUE MOULAY ISMAIL

RUE SIDI MIMOUN

7

RUE LALLA RIKANA

RUE BEN MARINE

RUE DOBA BEN WFAA

Petits Taxis ★

★ Asni Grands Taxis

M'hamid Shared Taxis

RUE IBN RACHID

Setti Fatma Shared Taxi Minibuses

Lagarb ★ Shared Taxis

Forex Bureau 7

DERB JDID

AVENUE HOUMAN EL FETOUAKI

6

Calèches ★

Petits Taxis ★ PLACE DES FERBLANTIER 9

ARSET EL HAJ 10

RUE ARSET EL MAACH (RUE D'ELECTRICITÉ)

Bitoun ✡ Synagogue

Bab Ech Charia

R. DOBA BEN WFAA

Bab Agnaou 11

Bab Mansour

Bab er Robb

Sidi es Soheili Cemetery

Les Bains de Marrakech

RUE DE LA KASBAH

Kasbah Mosque

Saadian Tombs 10

☾

El Badi Palace

KASBAH

12

13

ROUTE D'ASNI ET IMDGHENNAT

ROUTE DE L'OURIKA

RUE DE LA KASBAH

DERB LAKNABHA

RUE BAB MECHOUAR

DERB CHTOUKA

⊠ Bab Ksiba

DERB CHTOUKA

11

DERB CHTOUKA

DERB CHTOUKA

RUE DE BAB IRHLI

⊠ Bab Irhli

SHOPS	
Bazar du Musée	4
Chez Jakhla	10
El Louami Ahmed	5
Entreprise Bouchaib Complexe d'Artisanat	12
Jamade	2
Lantern shops	9
Les Enfants du Michelin	7
Mellah Market	8
Naturom	3
Nouredinne Boukhair	13
Original Design	6/11
Tamouziqua Mustapha Mimani	1

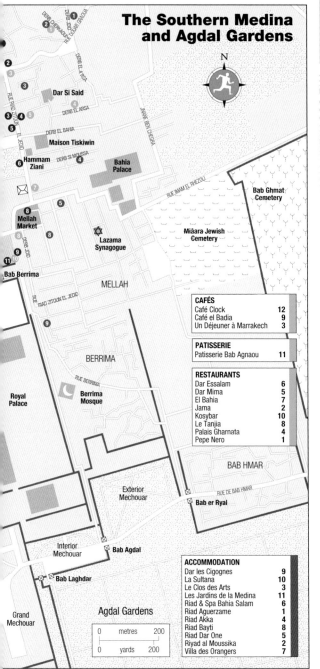

The Southern Medina and Agdal Gardens

N

Dar Si Said

Maison Tiskiwin

Hammam Ziani

Bahia Palace

Mellah Market

Lazama Synagogue

Bab Berrima

Bab Ghmat Cemetery

Miâara Jewish Cemetery

MELLAH

BERRIMA

Royal Palace

Berrima Mosque

Exterior Mechouar

Bab er Ryal

Interior Mechouar

Bab Agdal

Bab Laghdar

Grand Mechouar

Agdal Gardens

BAB HMAR

RUE DE BAB HMAR

CAFÉS
Café Clock	12
Café el Badia	9
Un Déjeuner à Marrakech	3

PATISSERIE
Patisserie Bab Agnaou	11

RESTAURANTS
Dar Essalam	6
Dar Mima	5
El Bahia	7
Jama	2
Kosybar	10
Le Tanjia	8
Palais Gharnata	4
Pepe Nero	1

ACCOMMODATION
Dar les Cigognes	9
La Sultana	10
Le Clos des Arts	3
Les Jardins de la Medina	11
Riad & Spa Bahia Salam	6
Riad Aguerzame	1
Riad Akka	4
Riad Bayti	8
Riad Dar One	5
Riyad al Moussika	2
Villa des Orangers	7

| 0 | metres | 200 |
| 0 | yards | 200 |

El Badi Palace

The Mellah

MAP p.54, POCKET MAP G7–J7

Set up in 1558, Marrakesh's **Jewish ghetto** was almost a town in itself in the sixteenth century, presided over by rabbis, and possessing its own souks, gardens, fountains and synagogues. Today it is almost entirely Muslim – most of the Jews left long ago for Casablanca, France or Israel.

The quarter is immediately distinct, with taller houses and narrower streets than elsewhere in the Medina. Would-be guides may offer (for a tip, of course) to show you some of the surviving synagogues, notably the **Lazama** at 36 Derb Ragraga (look for the cabal of faux guides hanging around outside; open to the public Mon–Thurs & Sun 9am–4pm, Fri 9am–1pm, closed Sat & Jewish hols; 10dh). The synagogue is still in use but the interior is modern and not tremendously interesting. Like all the Mellah's synagogues, it forms part of a private house, which you'll notice is decorated with Star of David zellij tiling. Just outside the Mellah, on Rue Arset el Mâach (Rue de l'Electricité), the first-floor **Bitoun Synagogue** is out of use and closed to the public,

but it's worth checking out the unusual mustard-yellow exterior, with a Star of David motif.

The **Miâara Jewish cemetery** on the east side of the Mellah (Mon–Thurs & Sun 8am–5pm, Fri 8am–1pm, closed Sat & Jewish hols; no charge but tip expected) is reckoned to date from the early seventeenth century. Among the tombs are eleven shrines to Jewish *marabouts* (*tzadikim*), illustrating an interesting parallel between the Moroccan varieties of Judaism and Islam.

El Badi Palace

MAP p.54, POCKET MAP G7

Bab Berrima. Daily 9am–5pm. 10dh.

Though largely ruined, and reduced throughout to its red *pisé* walls, enough remains of Sultan Ahmed el Mansour's sixteenth-century El Badi Palace to suggest that its name – "**The Incomparable**" – was not entirely immodest. The main courtyard that you see today was the ceremonial part of the palace complex, built for the reception of ambassadors and dignitaries, and not meant for everyday living.

The original entrance was in the southeast corner, but today you enter from the north, through the **Green Pavilion**, emerging into a vast **central courtyard** over 130m long and nearly as wide. In the northeast corner, you can climb up to get an overview from the ramparts and a closer view of the **storks** nesting atop them.

The central courtyard has four **sunken gardens**, each pair separated by a pool, with smaller pools in the four corners. When filled – as during the June Festival National des Arts Populaires (see p.122) – they are an incredibly majestic sight.

You can pay another 10dh (at the main entrance) to see the original **minbar** (pulpit) from the Koutoubia Mosque (see p.28), housed in a pavilion in the southwest corner of the main courtyard. Once one of the most celebrated works of art in the Muslim world, it was commissioned from Córdoba, the Andalusian capital, in 1137 ("al-Andalus" or Andalusia was under Islamic rule and had close links to Morocco from 711 until 1492; it was also the Islamic world's main artistic centre). The *minbar* took eight years to complete, and was covered with the most exquisite inlay work of which, sadly, only patches remain. South of the courtyard are the ruins of the **palace stables** and, beyond them, leading towards the walls of the present Royal Palace, a series of **dungeons**, used as a prison into the twentieth century.

As Ahmed's court jester quipped at the palace's inauguration, "Sire, this will make a magnificent ruin!"

Agdal Gardens

MAP p.54, POCKET MAP H8–J9
Access via the path leading south from the Interior Mechouar; bus #6 from Av Mohammed V near the Koutoubia will take you to the path's southern end, or take a taxi ☏ 0648 284465. Fri & Sun 7.30am–6pm. Free.

These massive gardens, which stretch south for some 3km, are surrounded by walls, with gates (which are kept closed) at each of the northern corners. Inside, the orange, fig, lemon, apricot and pomegranate **orchards** are divided up by raised walkways and broad avenues of olive trees. The area is watered by a system of wells and **underground channels**, known as *khettera*, that go as far as the foothills of the Atlas and date, in part, from the very founding of the city. These fell into disrepair, and the gardens were largely abandoned until the nineteenth century, when they were restored. The garden's containing walls were also built at that time.

At the heart of the gardens lies a series of pools, the largest of which is the **Sahraj el Hana**, the Tank of Health (now a green, algae-clogged rectangle of water). Probably dug during Almohad times, the pool is flanked by a ramshackle old **summer pavilion**, where the last few precolonial sultans held picnics and boating parties.

Summer pavilion, Agdal Gardens

Kasbah Mosque

MAP p.54, POCKET MAP G7
Place des Tombeaux Saadiens.

Originally Almohad, but rebuilt in the sixteenth century, the minaret of this mosque, with its wonderful green *darj w ktarf*, gives an idea of what the Koutoubia must have looked like in its heyday, when its stonework was covered by plaster and paint. Only Muslims may enter, but everybody can admire the exterior.

The Saadian Tombs

MAP p.54, POCKET MAP G7
Rue de la Kasbah. Daily 9am–4.45pm.
10dh.

The tombs of the Saadians – the dynasty that ruled Morocco from 1554 to 1669 – escaped plundering by the rapacious Sultan Moulay Ismail, of the subsequent Alaouite dynasty, probably because he feared bad luck if he desecrated them. Instead, he blocked all access bar an obscure entrance from the Kasbah Mosque. The tombs lay

Saadian Tombs

half-ruined and half-forgotten until they were rediscovered by a French aerial survey in 1917.

The finer of the two **mausoleums** in the enclosure is on the left as you come in – a beautiful group of three rooms. Architecturally, the most important feature here is the **mihrab**, its pointed horseshoe arch supported by an incredibly delicate arrangement of columns. The room itself was originally an oratory, probably not intended for burial use. Opposite the mihrab, an elaborate arch leads to the domed central chamber and the tomb of Sultan Ahmed el Mansour, flanked by those of his sons and successors. The room is spectacular, with faint light filtering onto the tombs from an interior lantern placed in the tremendous vaulted roof, and the zellij tilework on the walls full of colour and motion. It was Ahmed who built the other mausoleum, older and less impressive, above the tombs of his mother and of the Saadian dynasty's founder, Mohammed el Sheikh. Outside, round the garden and courtyard, are scattered the tombs of over a hundred more Saadian princes and members of the royal household.

The best time to visit is early in the morning, before the crowds arrive, or late in the afternoon when they – and the heat – have largely gone.

Bab Agnaou

MAP p.54, POCKET MAP F7
This was one of the two original entrances to the Kasbah, but the magnificent blue granite gateway that stands here today was built in 1885. The entrance is surrounded by concentric arches of decoration and topped with an inscription in decorative script, which translates as: "Enter with blessing, serene people."

Shops

Bazar du Musée

MAP p.54, POCKET MAP C13
Rue Riad Zitoun el Jedid ☏ 0671 842628.
Daily 10am–6pm.

Abdelkarim el Azri, who runs this shop, is a bit of a jack-of-all-trades, and he's got anything from babouches to scarfs if you want to buy them at good prices; however, what you really come here for are the range of tea glasses, from cheap and cheerful mass-produced to hand-blown in Majorelle blue – the colour of the pavillion in the Majorelle Garden (see p.64). He decorates many of these in hand-applied metal gilt, and if you need a pot to brew up in, he's got a few old ones for sale too.

Chez Jakha

MAP p.54, POCKET MAP G7
29 Arset el Haj. Mon–Thurs, Sat & Sun 9am–8pm.

The walls and floor here are stacked solid with CDs and cassettes of local and foreign sounds. There's Algerian *raï* and Egyptian pop, as well as homegrown *raï* and *chaabi* (folk music), classical Andalusian music originally from Muslim-era Spain, religious music and even Moroccan hip-hop.

El Louami Ahmed

MAP p.54, POCKET MAP C13
218 Rue Riad Zitoun el Jedid ☏ 0662 778347. Daily 10am–8pm.

If the leather babouches in the main souk don't wow you, pay a visit here for a whole different concept: women's babouches made from raffia straw, mainly candy-coloured, and there are ladies' sandals too. Ahmed sits in the shop making them by hand, so you can see him at work. A pair of simple babouches costs 150–300dh.

Entreprise Bouchaib Complexe d'Artisanat

Entreprise Bouchaib Complexe d'Artisanat

MAP p.54, POCKET MAP G8
7 Derb Baissi Kasbah, Rue de la Kasbah
☏ 0524 381853, ⓦ complexeartisanal.com.
Daily 8.30am–7pm.

A massive craftwork department store with a huge range of goods at (supposedly) fixed prices, only slightly higher than in the souks. The sales assistants who follow you round are generally quite charming and informative. Carpets are the best buy, at 2500–10,000dh for a decent-sized killim, or 5000–20,000dh for a knotted carpet. There's also a huge selection of jewellery, ceramics, brassware and even furniture.

Jamade

MAP p.54, POCKET MAP C13
1 Pl Douar Graoua, Rue Riad Zitoun el Jedid ☏ 0524 429042. Daily 10.30am–3pm & 4.30–7.30pm.

A chic little shop selling modern ceramics, as well as dresses, hats, bags and purses by local designers and co-ops, some interesting jewellery and some rather overpriced beauty products and perfumes. Best is their modern, designer take on the traditional Moroccan tea glass.

Lantern shops

MAP p.54, POCKET MAP H7
Pl des Ferblantiers. Daily 8am–7pm.

The stores on the eastern side of the square sell a big selection of brass and iron lanterns in all shapes and sizes, some with coloured glass panels, which make excellent light shades for electric bulbs. The many-pointed star-shaped lanterns with glass panes are a big favourite, as are simple candle-holder lanterns. There are larger and grander designs too, and these shops don't only sell them, but also make the lanterns on the premises, so you can watch the lantern-makers at work.

Les Enfants de Michelin

MAP p.54, POCKET MAP C13
84 Rue Riad Zitoun el Kedim ☎ 0656 184129. Daily 10am–9pm.

This is the latest and most imaginative in a group of shops that recycle disused tyres. Initially they made hammam supplies such as buckets and flip-flops (still sold at shop no.108, 50m down towards Pl des Ferblantiers), then picture frames and tuffets (try

Lanterns on Place des Ferblantiers

no.97, 25m down), but this shop makes clothes – a bit fetishy, but interesting – along with jewellery, purses and handbags. "Chic and intelligent recycling," they say, and you can't help but agree.

Mellah market

MAP p.54, POCKET MAP H7
Off Derb Jedid, by Pl des Ferblantiers. Daily 9am–7pm.

This is an interesting little market, especially for spices, which are piled up in attractively multicoloured and very photogenic pyramids. Other shops offer bowlfuls of glutinous traditional soap or rolls of rich fabric. Along with the rest of the Mellah, the market has been given something of a facelift and is now bright and clean, if perhaps not quite as atmospheric as it once was.

Naturom

MAP p.54, POCKET MAP C13
213 Rue Riad Zitoun el Jedid
☎ 0524 383784, ⓦ naturom.ma.
Daily 9.30am–8.30pm.

Naturom produce luscious cosmetics made with all kinds of fruits and natural ingredients, many grown on their own farm in the Atlas, and most of them are organic. There are appealing soaps, gels, creams, face cleansers made with ghassoul (natural mud shampoo) or activated charcoal, and even beard cream and oil.

Nouredinne Boukhair

MAP p.54, POCKET MAP G8
305 Rue de la Kasbah ☎ 0643 907634.
Mon–Thurs, Sat & Sun 10am–8pm, Fri 2–8pm.

This is the best among a handful of shops on this stretch of the street (there are imitators at nos. 315 and 297) that sell jolly little paintings on the wooden boards used by students in Koranic schools. They aren't exactly high art, but they're bright, breezy and original, and prices start around 100dh.

are lute-like *ginbris*, which make excellent souvenirs to hang on your wall back home.

Cafés

Café Clock

MAP p.54, POCKET MAP G8
224 Derb Chtouka, Kasbah ☏ 0524 378367, ⓦ marrakech.cafeclock.com. Daily 9am–11pm.

The super-cool Marrakesh branch of a well-known Fez café, this is a great place for breakfast (40dh), or a smoothie (30dh), or to try their famous camel burgers (95dh). In the evenings they have cultural events, including traditional storytelling in Arabic and English on Mondays and Thursdays, with music on other nights.

Café el Badia

MAP p.54, POCKET MAP H7
Off Pl des Ferblantiers, by Bab Berrima ☏ 0524 389975. Daily 9am–11pm.

On a rooftop looking out over Place des Ferblantiers and towards the Mellah, this is one place to get close to the storks nesting on the walls of the El Badi Palace. It serves a range of hot and cold (non-alcoholic) drinks, and set menus (100–130dh, including one vegetarian) featuring soup, salad, couscous, and Moroccan sweetmeats for afters.

Un Déjeuner à Marrakech

MAP p.54, POCKET MAP C13
2–4 Pl Douar Graoua, Rue Riad Zitoun el Jedid ☏ 0524 378387. Daily 11am–10pm.

Cool upmarket tearoom and restaurant serving teas and infusions, salads – think Caesar salad or salmon salad with blinis – and snacks (sandwiches, savoury tarts and crêpes). They also offer the odd main dish, usually involving a fusion of some kind, such as beef brochettes with stir-fried vegetables and sushi rice, and daily specials, generally in the 90–130dh range.

Camel burger at Café Clock

Original Design

MAP p.54, POCKET MAP C13 & H7
231 Rue Riad Zitoun el Jedid & 47 Pl des Ferblantiers ☏ 0524 383705, ⓦ originaldesign-marrakech.com. Daily 9.30am–7.30pm.

They started out making ceramics, but nowadays Original Design specializes in softer things, such as bags, clothes, table linen and foutah hammam towels, which make natty scarfs. The designs are unmistakeably Moroccan, but all with a modern touch, setting them apart from the run-of-the-mill versions elsewhere.

Tamouziqua Mustapha Mimani

MAP p.54, POCKET MAP C12
84 Kennaria Teoula, off Rue Riad Zitoun el Jedid ☏ 0671 518724. Daily 9am–8pm.

This small shop specializes in Moroccan musical instruments, most notably drums, which they make themselves in their neighbouring workshop, and Gnaoua castanets. Also on sale

Patisserie

Patisserie Bab Agnaou

MAP p.54, POCKET MAP F7
Bab Agnaou. Daily 9am–9pm.

Little more than a hole in
the wall – actually in the gate
(Bab Agnaou) itself – this little
patisserie serves nothing fancy,
just good, traditional Moroccan
sticky delights, mostly involving
nuts and filo pastry fried in syrup
on the premises. Even if you
don't want to buy a kilo of them,
a triangular *briouat* (filo parcel,
in this case filled with nuts),
perfumed with orange blossom
water, is irresistible, and a snip at
just 2dh.

Restaurants

Dar Essalam

MAP p.54, POCKET MAP C13
170 Rue Riad Zitoun el Kedim
☎ 0524 443520, ⓦ daressalam.com.
Daily noon–3pm & 8–11pm.

This seventeenth-century
mansion has five different salons,
all beautifully done out and
dripping with zellij and stucco.
Winston Churchill and Sean
Connery are among the past
diners here, and Doris Day and
James Stewart also ate here in
Hitchcock's *The Man Who Knew
Too Much*. The food (*menus
250–330dh plus wine) is good,
the ambience superb, and in the
evening there are musicians,
belly-dancers and Moroccan
Berber dancers.

Dar Mima

MAP p.54, POCKET MAP C13
9 Derb Zaouia el Khadiria, off Rue Riad
Zitoun el Jedid ☎ 0524 385252. Mon, Tues
& Thurs–Sun 8pm–midnight.

A modest nineteenth-century
townhouse converted into a
simple but comfortable restaurant
with the sort of food and
atmosphere that you might find

Patisserie Bab Agnaou

in a well-to-do Marrakshi family
home. The *menu* is 220dh per
person plus wine.

El Bahia

MAP p.54, POCKET MAP C13
1 Rue Riad Zitoun el Jedid, by the Bahia
Palace ☎ 0524 378679. Daily noon–10pm.

A proper palace restaurant,
but with bargain-priced 80dh
lunch dishes and 100dh supper
dishes. It's housed in a beautifully
restored mansion, complete with
finely carved stucco and painted
wooden ceilings, which used to
offer meals with a floorshow at
three times the price.

Jama

MAP p.54, POCKET MAP C12
149 Rue Riad Zitoun el Jedid ☎ 0524
429872. Daily 7am–10pm.

A quiet little patio, lit up with
candles in the evening, serving
a small selection of well-cooked
and modestly priced (50–60dh)
traditional tajines, including lamb
or beef with figs or prunes, and
chicken with lemons and olives,
followed by their own house
yoghurt.

Kosybar

MAP p.54, POCKET MAP H7
47 Pl des Ferblantiers ☎ 0524 380324,
🌐 kosybar.com. Daily 11am–1am.

This is a stylish restaurant and bar
with upstairs terraces overlooking
Place des Ferblantiers. At
lunchtime (until 4pm) there's a
150dh set menu or a choice of
light but exotic dishes such as
cabbage stuffed with Chinese
mushrooms. In the evening a full
à la carte menu is offered, with
dishes such as a seafood tajine
or roast duck breast with black
olives and fig jam, or you can go
for a lighter option in the form
of sushi. Main dishes are around
70–95dh at midday, 150–180dh in
the evening.

Le Tanjia

MAP p.54, POCKET MAP H7
14 Derb Jedid, by Pl des Ferblantiers
☎ 0657 733879, 🌐 letanjia-marrakech.
blogspot.com. Daily 1–11pm.

Stylish bar-restaurant, billed as
an "oriental brasserie", serving
well-cooked Moroccan dishes
(including vegetarian options)
in an old mansion with modern
decor. It's not outrageously
expensive – count on around
300dh per head plus wine.

Palais Gharnata

MAP p.54, POCKET MAP H6
5–6 Derb el Arsa, off Rue Riad Zitoun el
Jedid ☎ 0524 389615, 🌐 gharnata.com.
Daily 8–11pm.

This place is popular with foreign
visitors, though unfortunately the

Kosybar

Le Tanjia

food (the 550dh *menu* features
pastilla, couscous, lamb tajine
and wine) is merely so-so, and
individual diners play second
fiddle to groups. However, the
sixteenth-century mansion is
magnificently decorated, with an
Italian alabaster fountain at its
centre; scenes from *The Return
of the Pink Panther* were shot
here. Past patrons have included
Jacqueline Kennedy. There's a
floorshow (music and dancing)
from 8.30pm.

Pepe Nero

MAP p.54, POCKET MAP C12
Riyad al Moussika, 17 Derb Cherkaoui
(off Rue Douar Graoua) ☎ 0524 389067,
🌐 pepenero-marrakech.com. Tues–Sun
noon–2.30pm & 7.30–11pm.

The terrace and lounge of
the *Riyad al Moussika* make
an elegant venue for this
classy restaurant, serving fine
Moroccan and Italian food,
accompanied by Moroccan and
Italian wines. You can pick and
mix from the two cuisines, but
the Italian dishes are generally
the best. Main dishes 150–220dh.

The Ville Nouvelle and Palmery

The downtown area of Marrakesh's new town, the Ville Nouvelle, is Guéliz, whose main thoroughfare, Avenue Mohammed V, runs all the way down to the Koutoubia. It's in Guéliz that you'll find the more upmarket shops and most of Marrakesh's nightlife. South of Guéliz, the Hivernage district was built as a garden suburb, and is where most of the city's newer tourist hotels are located. Thoufgh the Ville Nouvelle is hardly chock-a-block with attractions, it does have one must-see: the Majorelle Garden, which is beautifully laid out with lily ponds, cactuses and a striking blue pavilion. West of Hivernage, the Menara Gardens are larger, greener and more like a park. Otherwise, you can get some peace and respite from the full-on activity of Marrakesh's streets by heading to the Palmery, or oasis, just outside the city.

Majorelle Garden (Jardin Bou Saf)

MAP OPPOSITE, POCKET MAP D2
Rue Yves Saint-Laurent (off Av Yacoub el Mansour) ☎ 0524 313047, ⓦ jardinmajorelle.com. Daily: May–Sept

Majorelle Garden

8am–6pm; Oct–April 8am–5.30pm; Ramadan 9am–5pm. 70dh; no dogs or unaccompanied children allowed.

The Majorelle Garden is a meticulously planned twelve-acre botanical garden, created in the 1920s and 1930s by French painter **Jacques Majorelle** (1886–1962). The feeling of tranquillity here is enhanced by verdant groves of bamboo, dwarf palm and agave, the cactus garden and the various lily-covered pools.

Majorelle's studio, a pavilion painted in a striking cobalt blue – the colour of French workmen's overalls, so Majorelle claimed – is now a **Berber Museum** (30dh), displaying traditional Berber crafts such as textiles and carpets, costumes and jewellery, and even an old wooden mosque pulpit.

The garden was subsequently owned by fashion designer **Yves Saint Laurent**, to whom a specially designed new museum in the garden is dedicated. Among its exhibits are two hundred outfits chosen from Saint Laurent's thousands of designs.

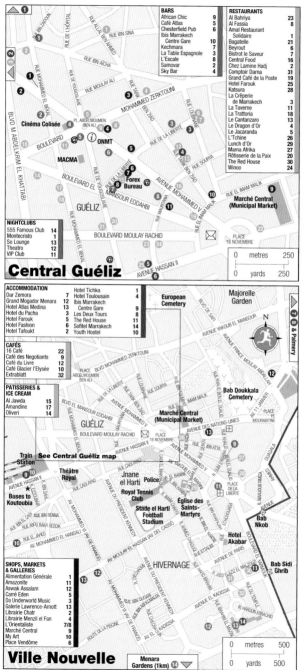

BARS

African Chic	9
Café Atlas	5
Chesterfield Pub	6
Ibis Marrakech Centre Gare	10
Kechmara	7
La Table Espagnole	3
L'Escale	8
Samovar	2
Sky Bar	4

RESTAURANTS

Al Bahriya	23
Al Fassia	8
Amal Restaurant Solidaire	1
Bagatelle	21
Beyrout	6
Bistrot le Saveur	7
Central Food	16
Chez Lamine Hadj	15
Comptoir Darna	31
Grand Café de la Poste	19
Hotel Farouk	25
Katsura	28
La Crêperie de Marrakech	3
La Taverne	11
La Trattoria	18
Le Cantanzaro	13
Le Dragon d'Or	4
Le Jacaranda	5
L'Tchine	26
Lunch d'Or	29
Mama Afrika	27
Rôtisserie de la Paix	20
The Red House	30
Winoo	24

NIGHTCLUBS

555 Famous Club	14
Montecristo	15
So Lounge	13
Theatro	12
VIP Club	11

Central Guéliz

ACCOMMODATION

Dar Zemora	7	Hotel Tichka	1
Grand Mogador Menara	12	Hotel Toulousain	4
Hotel Atlas Medina	13	Ibis Marrakech Centre Gare	9
Hotel du Pacha	3	Les Deux Tours	8
Hotel Farouk	5	The Red House	11
Hotel Fashion	6	Sofitel Marrakech	14
Hotel Tafoukt	2	Youth Hostel	10

CAFÉS

16 Café	22
Café des Negotiants	9
Café du Livre	12
Café Glacier l'Elysée	10
Extrablatt	32

PATISSERIES & ICE CREAM

Al Jawda	15
Amandine	17
Oliveri	14

SHOPS, MARKETS & GALLERIES

Alimentation Générale	1
Amazonite	11
Aswak Assalam	12
Carré Eden	5
Da Underworld Music	3
Galerie Lawrence-Arnott	13
Librairie Chatr	2
Librairie Menzil el Fan	4
L'Orientaliste	7/8
Marché Central	9
My Art	10
Place Vendôme	6

Ville Nouvelle

Minzah pavilion, Menara Gardens

Menara Gardens

MAP p.65, POCKET MAP A8–A9
Av de la Menara. Daily 7.30am–5pm. Free.

A popular picnic spot for Marrakshi families, the Menara Gardens couldn't be simpler to find: just follow the road from Bab Jedid, the gateway by the *Hotel La Mamounia*. The gardens are centred on a rectangular **pool** that provides a classic postcard image against a backdrop of the High Atlas mountains. Like the Agdal Gardens (see p.57), the Menara was restored and its pavilions rebuilt in the mid-nineteenth century, though unlike the Agdal it is more olive grove than orchard. The poolside **Minzah** pavilion (daily 9am–5pm; 10dh) replaced an earlier Saadian structure.

The gardens are served by bus #11 from the Koutoubia. There's usually someone opposite the park entrance offering camel rides for those wanting a little spin.

Avenue Mohammed V

MAP p.65, POCKET MAP B3–D5
Named after the king who presided over Morocco's independence from France, Avenue Mohammed V is Marrakesh's main artery. It's on and around this boulevard that you'll find the city's main concentration of upmarket shops, restaurants and smart pavement cafés, and its junctions form the Ville Nouvelle's main centres of activity: **Place de la Liberté**, with its modern fountain; **Place 16 Novembre**, by the main post office; and **Place Abdelmoumen Ben Ali**, focus of Marrakesh's modern shopping zone. Looking back along Avenue Mohammed V from Guéliz to the Medina, on a clear day at least, you should see the Koutoubia rising in the distance.

Église des Saints-Martyrs

MAP p.65, POCKET MAP C5
Rue de l'Imam Ali ☏ 0524 430585. Mon–Sat 6–7.30pm & Sun 10am–noon. Free.

Marrakesh's **Catholic church**, built in 1930, could easily be a little church in rural France but for its distinctly Marrakshi red-ochre hue. The church is dedicated to six Franciscan friars who insisted on preaching Christianity on the city's streets in the year 1220. When the sultan ordered them to either desist or leave, they refused, and were promptly beheaded, to be canonized by the Church in 1481.

MACMA (Musée d'Art et de Culture de Marrakech)

MAP p.65, POCKET MAP A14
34 Passage Ghandouri, 61 Rue Yougoslavie
☏ 0524 447379, ⓦ museemacma.com.
Mon –Sat 10am–7pm. 80dh.

This cool, modern gallery exhibits paintings of Marrakesh and Morocco by European artists from the colonial period, including Eugène Delacroix and Jacques Majorelle, along with contemporary paintings by Moroccan artists, plus a selection of classic photos of Marrakesh, antique painted doors and chests, ceramics and objets d'art. All in all, it's a fine collection.

The European Cemetery

MAP p.65, POCKET MAP C2
Rue Erraouda. Daily: April–Sept 7am–7pm; Oct–March 8am–6pm. Free.

Opened in 1925, the European Cemetery is a peaceful plot with lots of wild flowers, and some quite Poe-esque French family mausoleums. The first thing you'll notice on entry is the large white obelisk dedicated to the soldiers who fell fighting in Africa for Free France and democracy during

European Cemetery

World War II; 333 of these men have their last resting places in the cemetery's section H. The oldest part, to the left of the obelisk as you come in, contains the tombs of colonists from the 1920s and 1930s, most of whom seem to have been under 40 years old when they died.

The Palmery

MAP p.65, POCKET MAP J1
5km northeast of town, between the Route de Fès (N8) and the Route de Casablanca (N9).

Marrakesh's **Palmery** is dotted with the villas of prosperous Marrakshis, and also boasts a golf course and a couple of luxury hotels. The clumps of date palms look rather windswept, but the Palmery does have a certain tranquillity, and it's several degrees cooler than the Medina, which makes it a particular attraction in summer. Supposedly, it sprang from stones spat out by the date-munching troops of Marrakesh's founder, Youssef Ben Tachfine, but in fact the dates produced by its fifty thousand-odd palms are not of eating quality.

The most popular route through the oasis is the **Circuit de la Palmeraie**, which meanders through the trees and villas from the Route de Fès to the Route de Casablanca. The classic way to see it is by *calèche* (see p.114), and the sightseeing bus, the Marrakech Bus Touristique (see box, p.114), travels round it too. It's also possible to tour the Palmery on a camel – men by the roadside offer rides – or you could even do it on foot, though it's quite a long 5km stroll. As for public transport, the Route de Fès turn-off is served by bus #17, but the Route de Casablanca end is trickier, so it's best to take a cab up to that end to start, and finish at the Route de Fès, where there are more transport options.

Shops, markets and galleries

Alimentation Générale

MAP p.65, POCKET MAP A14
54 Av Mohammed V, at the corner of Rue Mohammed el Bekal, Guéliz ⓣ 0524 447182. Mon–Sat 9am–8pm, Sun 11am–8pm.

Forget the groceries – they're just a front for what this place really sells, which is booze. Among the spirits, the stuff in what looks like a Ricard bottle is popular locally, but best avoided. Moroccan wines, mostly red, are variable, but the top choices are CB or Chateau Roslane, at 220dh a bottle, followed by Medaillon (120dh) and Domaine de Sahari (60dh). Among the cheap brands (40–50dh), Cabernet and Ksar are usually quite drinkable.

Amazonite

MAP p.65, POCKET MAP B15
94 Bd el Mansour Eddahbi, Guéliz ⓣ 0524 449926. Mon–Sat 10am–1.30pm & 4–7.30pm.

The Marrakesh branch of a Casablanca shop long known for its fine stock of *objets d'art*, Amazonite is the product of the owner's passion for rare and beautiful things. Most of the pieces are antique, with a hefty proportion comprising jewellery; if asked, staff will explain each item with charm and grace.

Aswak Assalam

MAP p.65, POCKET MAP E3
Av 11 Janvier at the junction with Av Prince Moulay Abdallah, Guéliz ⓣ 0524 431004. Daily 8am–11pm.

This smallish hypermarket may not be the most atmospheric shop in town, but it is quick and easy. There's a good patisserie section, and serve-yourself grains and spices, so you can weigh out exactly how much you want. You'll also find a fuller (and probably fresher) range of dairy products than you would at a grocery store, and there are even household items like kitchen wares, including couscous steamers.

Carré Eden Shopping Center

MAP p.65, POCKET MAP B14
Av Mohammed V at Rue de la Liberté ⓣ 0524 437246, ⓦ carreedenshoppingcenter.com. Carrefour daily 9am–10pm; other shops Mon–Thurs & Sun 10am–9pm, Fri & Sat 10am–10pm; food court Mon–Thurs & Sun 10am–11pm, Fri & Sat 10am–midnight.

A downtown shopping mall where you'll find lots of international designer clothes stores, plus one or two Moroccan ones. Down in the basement, there's a Carrefour supermarket, which is very handy for groceries. There's also a food court on the upper floor, in case you need some junk fast food, and, more enticingly, a branch of *Oliveri* (see p.71) outside the main entrance.

Da Underworld Music

MAP p.65, POCKET MAP B14
Rue Tarik Ben Ziad, Guéliz ⓣ 0524 423881. Daily 11am–10pm.

A good selection of Moroccan and Arabic music, with lots of Gnaoua, *raï* and Moroccan dance and

Amazonite

hip-hop CDs at 15dh a go. However, there's also a section for Western music, not exactly up-to-the-minute, but you can still turn up some great bargains.

Galerie Lawrence-Arnott

MAP p.65, POCKET MAP D4
Immeuble el Khalil, Av des Nations-Unies, Guéliz ☎ 0524 430999. Mon–Fri 10am–12.30pm & 3–7pm, Sat 10am–12.30pm.

Very upmarket gallery founded by two London art dealers, friends of Princess Diana and already well established on the London art scene when they opened a gallery in Tangier. This is their second Moroccan locale. The paintings and sculptures, as you might expect, are very fine and very expensive (nothing under 5000dh), but if you want to see what's really big on the Moroccan art scene, this is the place to come.

Librairie Chatr

MAP p.65, POCKET MAP A14
19 Av Mohammed V, Guéliz ☎ 0524 447997.
Mon–Thurs 8.30am–1pm & 3–8pm, Fri 8.30am–1pm & 3.30–8pm, Sat 8.30am–1pm & 4–9pm.

This bookshop and stationer sells mainly French titles, but there's also a shelf of English-language material, mostly classics, at the back on the right. The front part of the shop supplies artists' materials, as well as a large and varied selection of pens.

Librairie Menzil el Fan

MAP p.65, POCKET MAP A14
Résidence Tayeb, 55 Bd Mohammed Zerktouni, Guéliz ☎ 0524 446792. Mon–Sat 9am–12.30pm & 3–7pm.

This bookshop stocks the beautiful ACR range of French art and coffee-table books, which include several on Marrakesh and Moroccan interior design. There are also books on subjects such as architecture, textiles and jewellery, and cooking (though mostly in French) and even greetings cards.

L'Orientaliste

L'Orientaliste

MAP p.65, POCKET MAP B14
11 & 15 Rue de la Liberté, Guéliz ☎ 0524 434074. Mon–Sat 9am–1pm & 3–7pm, Sun 9am–12.30pm.

Specializing in chic North African-style home furnishings (though some are Syrian), L'Orientaliste also does a fine line in traditional ceramics from Fez and old Moroccan film posters. The stock at no. 11 is mainly furniture, while at no. 15 they concentrate on smaller items, including glassware and their own perfume.

Marché Central (Municipal Market)

MAP p.65, POCKET MAP C4
Rue Ibn Toumert, Guéliz. Daily 7am–8pm, though individual shops may keep shorter hours, and most close Fri or Sun.

A far cry from the souks in the Medina, this covered market is where expats and better-off Marrakshis come for their fresh fish, meat, fruit and veg. There are two butchers selling horsemeat, one selling pork, and shops specializing in pickled lemons, perfumed soaps, fossils, ceramics, booze, tourist tat and flowers.

My Art

MAP p.65, POCKET MAP B15
Rue Saint Aulaire by Pl 16 Novembre
℡ 0524 449181. Mon–Sat 9.30am–1.30pm
& 3.30–7.30pm.

Modern art and design, all made in Marrakesh, with everything from sculpture and paintings to furniture, soft toys and decorative *objets d'art*. The shop is a cool exhibition space that's worth a look just to see what they've got. This is the modern, chic side of Marrakesh, a far cry from the traditional crafts on sale in the Medina, but actually just as exciting, and with fixed prices.

Place Vendôme

MAP p.65, POCKET MAP B14
141 Av Mohammed V, Guéliz ℡ 0524
435263. Mon–Sat 9am–1pm & 3–7pm.

Moroccan leather is world famous, and you'll find plenty of it here including some very sumptuous soft leather and suede, in the form of bags, belts, wallets and clothes. Small purses start at 100dh, and there are some very stylish ladies' garments – jackets and dresses – at around 5000dh.

Place Vendôme

Cafés

16 Café

MAP p.65, POCKET MAP C4
Pl 16 Novembre, Guéliz ℡ 0524 339670,
Ⓦ 16cafe.com. Daily 8am–11pm.

There are coffees, teas and infusions on offer at this cool, elegant café, not to mention hot chocolate, ice cream and amazing pastries. It's located in a new shopping development, and the cuisine is even more modern than the simple, stylish decor. There are salads and sandwiches, quiches and even beer and wine. Main dishes go for 95–155dh.

Café des Negotiants

MAP p.65, POCKET MAP A14
Pl Abdelmoumen Ben Ali ℡ 0524 422345.
Daily 6am–10pm.

Slap-bang on the busiest corner in Guéliz, this grand café has been going since 1936 and it's *the* place to sit out on the pavement and really feel that you're in the heart of modern Marrakesh. It's also an excellent venue in which to spend the morning over a coffee, with an omelette (12dh) or sandwich (18–23dh) to accompany your caffeine fix.

Café du Livre

MAP p.65, POCKET MAP B14
44 Rue Tarik Ben Ziad, by Hotel Toulousain,
Guéliz ℡ 0524 432149. Mon–Sat 11.30am–
midnight.

A very elegant space, serving tea and coffee, juices, breakfasts, salads, sandwiches and brochettes, even tapas (well, mezze) at 25dh a go, or three for 70dh and toasties (25–30dh). There's also draught beer. The café also has a library of secondhand English books to read or buy, and free wi-fi too.

Café Glacier l'Élysée

MAP p.65, POCKET MAP A14
8 Bd Mohammed Zerktouni, next to the
CTM office. Daily 6am–11pm.

You need only wander less than 200m off Avenue Mohammed V to slice a third off the price of your coffee, as you will if you eschew the glitzy cafés on the main thoroughfare in favour of this Moroccan coffee house. It's nothing special, but that's the point: the coffee's just as good, so are the croissants, and all that's missing is the chic, Frenchified ambience.

Extrablatt

MAP p.65, POCKET MAP D6
Rue Echchouada, at the corner with Av el Kadissia, Hivernage ☎ 0524 435043. Daily 8am–midnight.
Spacious and modern upmarket café with an outside terrace, the Marrakesh branch of a German franchise chain, where you can get a range of set breakfasts (49–90dh), sandwiches, salads, coffees, sodas, juices, mocktails and light meals, including a couple of vegetarian options. If you're in Hivernage, it's something of an oasis.

Patisseries and ice cream

Al Jawda (Chez Mme Alami)

MAP p.65, POCKET MAP B15
11 Rue de la Liberté, Guéliz ☎ 0524 433897. Mon–Sat 8am–8.30pm, Sun 9am–6pm.
A refined patisserie, patronized by Marrakesh's high society and expatriate community. A fine selection of mouthwatering Moroccan pastries are on offer, including almond-filled petits fours such as crescent-shaped cornes de gazelle. It's a bit pricey, but is also very good.

Amandine

MAP p.65, POCKET MAP A15
177 Rue Mohammed el Bekal, Guéliz ☎ 0524 449612, ✉ amandinemarrakech.com. Daily 7am–9pm.

Café du Livre

An elegant café-patisserie, stuffed full of scrumptious almond-filled Moroccan pastries and French-style cream cakes, where you can relax with a coffee and your choice of sweetmeat. The Moroccan sweets include cornes de gazelle (almond-filled crescents) and – their speciality – macaroons, in a variety of flavours, including vanilla, chocolate, strawberry, pistachio and salted caramel although they're admittedly a bit pricey at 7dh each.

Oliveri

MAP p.65, POCKET MAP A15
Bd el Mansour Eddahbi, behind Hotel Agdal, Guéliz ☎ 0524 449913. Daily 8am–midnight.
The Marrakesh branch of a Casablanca firm that's been serving delicious, creamy, Italian-style ices since colonial times, this is the poshest ice-cream parlour in town. You can eat your scoop from a proper ice-cream goblet among elegant surroundings, accompanied, should you so desire, by coffee; or else you can take it away in a waffle cone. They have an even more central branch outside Carré Eden mall (see p.68) on Avenue Mohammed V.

Restaurants

Al Bahriya

MAP p.65, POCKET MAP B15
75 Bis Bd Moulay Rachid, Guéliz ☎ 0661
242047. Daily 11am–midnight.

Very cheap and very popular fish restaurant, always crowded out at lunchtimes. For 50dh you get a big plate of hake, sole and squid, plus bread, olives and sauce, or for not much more there are swordfish brochettes, fish tajines, fried prawns and fish soup. Unbeatable value.

Al Fassia

MAP p.65, POCKET MAP B14
Résidence Tayeb, 55 Bd Mohammed
Zerktouni, Guéliz ☎ 0524 434060,
W alfassia.com. Mon & Wed–Sun
noon–2.30pm & 7.30–11pm.

Al Fassia is truly Moroccan – both in decor and cuisine – and specializes in dishes from the country's culinary capital, Fez. Start with that great Fassi classic, pigeon pastilla, followed by a choice of nine different tajines, or any of the other sumptuous Fassi offerings. Expect to pay around 350dh, more with wine. If you want to sample the very best traditional Moroccan cooking, with superb ambience and service, this is the place.

Amal Restaurant Solidaire

MAP p.65, POCKET MAP A14
Rue Allal Ben Ahmed at Rue Ibn Sina
☎ 0524 446896, W amalnonprofit.org.
Daily noon–4pm.

A non-profit self-help organization for disadvantaged women where training in the catering trade is put to good use in this lunchtime restaurant. What exactly's on offer changes from day to day, but there's always a tasty tajine (35dh), often brochettes (45dh) and usually cakes and pastries too. You can also participate in a cookery workshop (daily except Fri

Amal Restaurant Solidaire

10am–noon), and then eat what you cooked.

Bagatelle

MAP p.65, POCKET MAP A15
103 Rue de Yougoslavie ☎ 0524 430274,
W bagatelle-marrakech.com. Daily
9am–3pm & 7–11pm.

Photos of Marrakesh in the 1950s deck the walls, and there's a lovely vine-shaded garden to eat in at this French-style bistro which first opened its doors in 1949. You can start with an entrée such as pork and guinea fowl terrine, take in some braised veal tongue in caper sauce, and round it off with a refreshing sorbet. Throw in a coffee or a mint tea, and you'll be paying around 250dh per head.

Beyrout

MAP p.65, POCKET MAP B14
10 Rue Loubnane, Guéliz ☎ 0524 423525.
Daily noon–3pm & 7pm–midnight.

A Lebanese restaurant serving typical Middle Eastern cuisine, starting off, naturally, with cold mezze (hors d'oeuvres) such as hummus, *moutabbel* (aubergine and tahini dip) and tabbouleh, and hot starters such as falafel, *kubbe* (a fried bulgur wheat ball with a meat and onion filling), and even moussaka. You can get a selection of eight mezze for 265dh, twelve for 390dh, and if you've still got room after that, mains go for 70–120dh. Licensed.

Bistrot le Saveur

MAP p.65, POCKET MAP B14
Le Caspien Hotel, 12 Rue Loubnane, Guéliz ☏ 0524 422282. Daily noon–11pm.

Opposite the end of Rue de la Liberté, this is a modest little restaurant serving a selection of international dishes, mostly French or Moroccan, but there are also pizzas, pasta dishes and risottos. All are good, and quite moderately priced, with main dishes at 120–160dh. Licensed.

Central Food

MAP p.65, POCKET MAP B15
172 Av Mohammed ☏ 0524 420537. Daily 7am–midnight.

It looks like a plastic fast-food joint but this popular and very reasonably priced diner is much better than that. True, the "tacos" bear no relation to their Mexican namesake, but most dishes are good and freshly prepared. You can choose your own fish and have it served with chips (50dh), or pop in for breakfast (25–50dh) or just a juice or a salad. On Fridays they even have couscous (40dh).

Chez Lamine

MAP p.65, POCKET MAP A2
19 Résidence Yasmine, Rue Ibn Aïcha, corner with Rue Mohammed el Bekal, Guéliz ☏ 0524 431164. Daily noon–midnight.

Unpretentious, inexpensive restaurant (main dishes 50–70dh) which is very popular with Marrakshis for *mechoui* (roasts), grills, tajines, sheep's head, brochettes and other indigenous, mainly lamb-based dishes.

Comptoir Darna

MAP p.65, POCKET MAP D6
Rue Echchouada, Hivernage ☏ 0524 437702, ⊕ comptoirmarrakech.com. Daily 7pm–3am (food served 8pm–1am).

Downstairs it's a restaurant serving reliably good Moroccan and international cuisine, with main courses at 165–250dh, and dishes such as seafood tajine, salmon steak or weeping tiger (steak in ginger sauce), as well as one or two vegetarian options. Upstairs it's a chic lounge bar, very popular with Marrakesh's young and rich. The bar opens at 7pm, with meals served from 8pm, and cabaret entertainment starting at 10.30pm.

Grand Café de la Poste

MAP p.65, POCKET MAP B15
Rue el Imam Malik, just off Av Mohammed V behind the post office, Guéliz ☏ 0524 433038, ⊕ grandcafedelaposte.restaurant. Daily 8am–1am.

More grand than café, this is in fact quite a posh restaurant – France's colonial governor T'hami el Glaoui used to dine here back in the day – serving international cuisine. The menu, which changes quite regularly, includes a selection of beef, duck and fish dishes, and main courses mostly go for 160–260dh. For drinks, you can wash it down with a cup of Earl Grey, or there's a choice of rums, tequilas and fine brandies if you prefer something harder.

Grand Café de la Poste

Hotel Farouk

MAP p.65, POCKET MAP B15
66 Av Hassan II, Guéliz ☏ 0524 431989.
Daily 5am–midnight.

From noon the hotel restaurant offers an excellent-value 35–45dh set menu with soup or salad, then couscous, tajine or brochettes, followed by fruit or home-made yoghurt. Alternatively, tuck into one of their excellent wood-oven pizzas (30–40dh).

Katsura

MAP p.65, POCKET MAP D4
1 Rue Oum Errabia, Guéliz ☏ 0524 434358,
🌐 katsura.ma. Daily noon–2.30pm &
7.30–11.30pm.

Billing itself as a "Thai wok and sushi restaurant", this is Marrakesh's first Thai restaurant, and it's not at all bad, with the usual Thai standards including green or red curries (75–100dh), plus Japanese snacks, mainly sushi (35–50dh), and set menus (100dh lunchtime, 200dh evening). The food's fresh and tasty, and the service is pleasant and efficient. All in all, a nice change from the usual Marrakesh fare.

La Crêperie de Marrakech

MAP p.65, POCKET MAP A2
14 Rue Petit Marché de Guéliz, off Route
de Targa, Guéliz ☏ 0524 432208. Mon–Sat
noon–3pm & 6–10pm.

Crêpes, naturally – Breton-style ones, apparently – with a choice of sweet or savoury fillings. The latter (40–60dh) include spinach and white cheese, or Roquefort, or egg and chorizo. Among the sweet fillings (20–50dh), there's apple with cinnamon, or chestnut cream, or the classic crêpe Suzette (with Grand Marnier liqueur).

La Taverne

MAP p.65, POCKET MAP A14
22 Bd Mohammed Zerktouni, Guéliz
☏ 0524 446126. Daily noon–3pm &
7.30–11pm.

As well as a drinking tavern, this is a pretty decent restaurant – in

La Crêperie de Marrakech

fact, it claims to be the oldest in town – where you can dine on French and Moroccan food indoors or in a lovely tree-shaded garden. The 130dh set menu isn't bad value either.

La Trattoria

MAP p.65, POCKET MAP A15
179 Rue Mohammed el Bekal, Guéliz
☏ 0524 432641, 🌐 latrattoriamarrakech
.com. Daily noon–3pm & 7pm–midnight;
bar noon–1am.

La Trattoria serves the best Italian food in town, with impeccable, friendly service and excellent cooking. The restaurant is located in a 1920s house decorated by the acclaimed American designer Bill Willis. As well as freshly made pasta, steaks and escalopes, there's beef medallions in Parmesan – the house speciality – plus a wonderful tiramisu to squeeze in for afters. Expect to pay about 400dh, more with wine.

Le Cantanzaro

MAP p.65, POCKET MAP B14
50 Rue Tarik Ben Ziad, Guéliz ☏ 0524
433731. Mon–Sat noon–2.30pm &
7.15–11pm.

This is one of the city's most popular Italian restaurants, crowded at lunchtime and suppertime alike with Marrakshis, expats and tourists. Specialities include *saltimbocca alla romana* and rabbit in mustard sauce, and there's crème brûlée or tiramisu to round it off with. It's licensed but not that expensive (main dishes are 90–120dh, pizzas and pasta 55–70dh). It's always best to book, but you can also just turn up and queue for a table if you don't mind waiting.

Le Dragon d'Or

MAP p.65, POCKET MAP B14
82 Bd Mohammed Zerktouni, Guéliz
☎ 0524 430617. Daily noon–2pm & 7–11pm.

A pick'n'mix of East Asian cuisine, with bright and cheerful decor, *Le Dragon d'Or* is popular with local families and there's a takeaway service. Dishes include traditional Chinese takeaway favourites (chow mein, sweet and sour and the like), quite a few duck dishes, and a handful of Vietnamese dishes, plus sushi

Lunch d'Or

for good measure. Main dishes are 90–135dh, and there's a 180dh lunchtime set menu. Licensed.

Le Jacaranda

MAP p.65, POCKET MAP A14
32 Bd Mohammed Zerktouni, Guéliz
☎ 0524 447215. Daily noon–3pm & 7.30–11pm.

The traditional French cuisine at *Le Jacaranda* is always reliably good. Start perhaps with renowned oysters from Oualidia on the coast (in the form, if you like, of oyster brochettes with smoked duck breast), beef carpaccio, or snails in garlic butter, and follow it with medallions or tournedos of beef, or grilled sea bass flambéed in pastis. À la carte eating will set you back around 330dh a head plus wine; alternatively, there are 100dh, 159dh and 297dh lunchtime set menus (but only the 159dh and 297dh menus in the evening).

L'Tchine

MAP p.65, POCKET MAP C4
Ave des Nations Unies at Rue Badr
☎ 0524 438980, ⓦ ltchine-restaurant.com.
Daily 7am–11.30pm.

A good spot to call by for breakfast, lunch or supper, in bright and breezy surrounds, where the food is as slow-cooked and traditional as a fish tajine (80dh) or Marrakshi tanjia (95dh), or as fast and modern as a cheese bagel breakfast with yoghurt and OJ (40dh).

Lunch d'Or

MAP p.65, POCKET MAP D5
Rue de l'Imam Ali, Guéliz. Daily 8am–7.30pm.

It can be hard to find honest-to-goodness cheap Moroccan food in the Ville Nouvelle, but this place is one of a pair opposite the church serving tasty tajines at 25dh a shot, as well as salads and brochettes. Great value and very popular with workers on their lunch break.

Mama Afrika

MAP p.65, POCKET MAP D4
3 Rue Oum Errabia ☎ 0524 457382.
Daily 24hr.

Done out like a cabaña on some tropical beach, *Mama Afrika* serves coffee, snacks, juices and dishes with an African-Caribbean flavour. In fact, they serve everything except alcohol, but there are tasty mocktails, and reggae music to get you in that dancing mood. Main courses 40–55dh.

Rôtisserie de la Paix

MAP p.65, POCKET MAP B15
68 Rue de Yougoslavie, alongside the former Cinema Lux-Palace, Guéliz ☎ 0524 433118, ⓦ rotisseriedelapaix.com. Daily noon–3pm & 7.30pm–midnight.

An open-air grill, established in 1949, specializing in mixed grills barbecued over wood, usually with a fish option. It's all served either in a salon, which has a roaring fire in winter, or in the shaded garden in summer. Couscous is served on Fridays only. A meal here will set you back around 120dh per head, not including wine.

The Red House

MAP p.65, POCKET MAP E6
Bd el Yarmouk, opposite the Medina wall, Hivernage ☎ 0524 437040 or ☎ 0524 437041, ⓦ theredhousemarrakech.com. Daily noon–3pm & 8–11.30pm.

You'll need to reserve ahead to eat at this palatial riad, which is beautifully decorated in stucco and zellij. There are Moroccan dishes such as lamb tajine with prunes and sesame (180dh) or international choices such as seafood risotto (190dh), all accompanied by music and belly-dancing. Desserts include sweet pastilla or apple tart with licorice ice cream. Licensed.

Winoo

MAP p.65, POCKET MAP B15
77 Bd Moulay Rachid (at Rue Mauritania) ☎ 0524 430400. Daily 7am–3am.

The Red House

A justifiably popular café-restaurant where you can stop by for a juice or a smoothie (the avocado and almond is especially delicious), a huge salad or a tasty tajine (the usual options, but also things like shrimp), all freshly made, well presented and very inexpensive (a meal won't cost much more than 70dh). It gets very busy at mealtimes but that isn't exactly surprising.

Bars

African Chic

MAP p.65, POCKET MAP D4
6 Rue Oum Errabia, Guéliz. ☎ 0524 431424, ⓦ africanchic-marrakech.com. Daily 8pm–4am.

One of Marrakesh's most congenial bars, *African Chic* is informal and relaxed, with cocktails, wines, beers, tapas (five for 70dh, eight for 100dh), salads, pasta, and meat and fish dishes. Live Latin and Gnaoua music every night from 10pm.

Café Atlas

MAP p.65, POCKET MAP A14
Place Abdelmoumen Ben Ali, Guéliz
☎ 0524 448888. Daily 10am–11pm.

A pavement café in the very centre
of Guéliz, but wander inside,
and hey presto, it is magically
transformed into a bar, with
bottled beer, spirits and plates
of bar snacks on the counter.
In theory, you could take your
drink out on the pavement,
but that would be considered
rather indiscreet, so it's best to
remain within, where respectable
passers-by won't notice that you're
indulging in alcohol.

Chesterfield Pub

MAP p.65, POCKET MAP B14
Hotel Nassim, 119 Av Mohammed V, Guéliz
☎ 0524 446401. Tues, Wed, Fri & Sat
noon–1am, Mon, Thurs & Sun 3pm–1am.

Upstairs in the *Hotel Nassim*,
this supposedly English-style
pub is one of Marrakesh's more
sophisticated watering holes, with
a cosy if rather smoky bar area,
all soft seats and muted lighting.
There's also a more relaxed, open-
air poolside terrace on which to
lounge with your draught beer or
cocktail of a summer evening.

Ibis Marrakech Centre Gare

MAP p.65, POCKET MAP A4
Av Hassan II, by the old train station
entrance, Guéliz ☎ 0524 435936.
Daily 24hr.

This hotel bar is not the most
atmospheric bar in town – just an
area of the lobby, it has no feeling
of intimacy at all. Nonetheless,
it has the advantage of being
a place where women can feel
comfortable having a quiet drink
or two.

Kechmara

MAP p.65, POCKET MAP B15
3 Rue de la Liberté, Guéliz ☎ 0524 422532,
ⓦ kechmara.com. Mon–Sat 11.30am–1am.

Downstairs, *Kechmara* is a cool
bar-café with a slightly Japanese
feel; upstairs there's an alfresco
terrace with a contemporary
design. A hip place to hang out,
with modern art exhibitions and
live music (soul, jazz and funk)
on the terrace (Wed & Fri evenings
from 8.30pm), it also serves food
including burgers (110dh), fish
and chips (110dh) and, from
6.30pm nightly, tapas.

La Table Espagnole

MAP p.65, POCKET MAP B14
34 Rue de la Liberté ☎ 0661 211225,
ⓦ facebook.com/pg/latableespagnole.
Daily 11pm–5am.

A bar specializing in tapas
(20–50dh) and *pinchos* (Basque
tapas), largely seafood-based,
although they'll happily dish you
up a portion of *patatas bravas*
(potato wedges doused in chilli
sauce) along with your *pulpo a la
gallega* (Galician-style octopus).
The beers and wines are Moroccan
rather than Spanish, but they
compensate with a decent paella,
and they show La Liga matches on
the TV screens.

Kechmara

L'Escale

MAP p.65, POCKET MAP B15
Rue Mauritanie, just off Av Mohammed V,
Guéliz ☏ 0524 433447. Daily 11am–11pm.

A down-at-heel, spit-and-sawdust
kind of bar, this place has been
going since 1947 and specializes
in good bar snacks, such as fried
fish or spicy merguez sausages
– you could even come here for
lunch or dinner (there's a dining
area at the back). The interior isn't
recommended for unaccompanied
women, especially in the evening,
but there's a family-friendly (no
booze) terrace for eating out front
by day.

Samovar

MAP p.65, POCKET MAP A14
145 Rue Mohammed el Bekal, Guéliz, next
to the Hotel Oudaya, Guéliz. ☏ 0661
249423. Daily 8am–10pm.

Samovar is an old-school, low-life
drinking den; a male hangout
with bar girls in attendance. The
customers get more and more out
of it as the evening progresses – if
you want to see the underbelly
of Morocco's drinking culture,
this is the place. Definitely not
recommended for womens
visitors, however.

Sky Bar

MAP p.65, POCKET MAP A14
Renaissance Hotel, Place Abdelmoumen
Ben Ali, Guéliz ☏ 0524 337777. Daily
10pm–1am.

Colonial-era building regulations
help keep the city's skyline down
to five stories, but somehow the
Renaissance Hotel, smack-bang in
the middle of downtown Guéliz,
escaped the limitation and its
seventh-floor rooftop bar thus has
the best view in town. Although a
beer here will cost you 60dh, the
bar's terrace is by far Marrakesh's
top spot to sip one while watching
the sun set.

Nightclubs

555 Famous Club

MAP p.65, POCKET MAP D9
Hotel Ushuaïa Clubbing, Bd Mohammed VI,
Aguedal ☏ 0678 181085, ⓦ beachclub555.
com. Daily 11pm–5am. Entry 200–300dh
(women usually free).

The Marrakesh branch of a famous
Tangier beach club. It's pricey – to
get in, to get a drink, to use the
cloakroom – but most nights
are "ladies' night", so women go

Sky Bar

free, and in principle get certain drinks free too, although they may give you the runaround on that. Music is a mix of electronic dance, hip-hop and Arabic hits, and the crowd are also very mixed. There's quite a lot of prostitution, and no photos are allowed, a rule that's rigorously policed.

Montecristo

MAP p.65, POCKET MAP B2
20 Rue Ibn Aïcha, Guéliz ☏ 0661 244912,
Ⓦ montecristomarrakech.com.
Daily 7pm–4am. Free entry.

Four spaces in one: a stylishly decorated restaurant serving decent if not outstanding food; a pub with live music from 11pm and a Cuban theme including (naturally) Montecristo cigars; a nightclub with DJs playing Arabic and Western dance sounds; and a rooftop "*Sky Bar*", where you can puff on *sheesha* pipes or Havana cigars. Sex workers are evident, but aside from that it's quite a posh joint, and the smoking terrace is an excellent chill-out zone.

So Lounge

MAP p.65, POCKET MAP D6
Sofitel Marrakesh, Rue Haroun Errachid,
Hivernage ☏ 0656 515009. Daily
7pm–4am. Entry 200–250dh.

This lounge bar, restaurant and nightclub combo has become one of the trendiest venues in town, catering to an extremely well-coiffed, jet-set crowd. You'll find everyone from the Marrakshi elite to weekending yacht owners in from the Riviera. Regular live acts (9.30pm–midnight) play everything from rock to *raï* – the French-based group Alabina, for example – after which the dancefloor opens up to the sounds of house and dub DJs. Dress to impress or you won't get in.

Theatro

MAP p.65, POCKET MAP D6
Hotel es Saadi, Av el Kadissia (also spelt
Qadassia), Hivernage ☏ 0524 448811,

So Lounge

Ⓦ theatromarrakech.com. Daily 11.30pm–4am. Entry 200dh (Mon–Thurs & Sun) to 300dh (Fri & Sat).

One of Marrakesh's more interesting nightclubs, located in, as its name suggests, an old theatre. Nights are themed (ladies' night on Tuesdays, for example, and hip-hop night on Thursdays) and the atmosphere is sophisticated – though make no mistake, by the early hours the crowd are really going for it. Music is the usual mix of house, trance, techno and r'n'b with Algerian *raï* and Middle Eastern pop, but the special effects and circus-style performers on stage make it a cut above most Marrakesh clubs.

VIP Club

MAP p.65, POCKET MAP D5
Place de la Liberté, Guéliz. Daily: bar
8pm–4am; club midnight–4am ☏ 0661
152026.

Stairs lead down from the entrance to the first level, where there's a lounge bar, with happy hour until 11pm, and then (from midnight) further down to the deepest level, where there's what the French call a *boîte*, meaning a sweaty little nightclub. It's got a circular dancefloor and a small bar area, but despite its diminutive size, the place rarely seems to be full.

Atlas excursions

The countryside around Marrakesh is some of the most beautiful in Morocco. The High Atlas mountains that make such a spectacular backdrop to the city are even more impressive when you're actually among them. For a spot of hiking, or even skiing, they're easy enough to reach in an hour or two by grand taxi, usually from Place Youssef Tachfine (Sidi Mimoun), south of the Koutoubia. Imlil is the best base for mountain treks, but Setti Fatma, in the beautiful Ourika Valley, is more picturesque, and handier for less strenuous walking, while Oukaïmeden is Morocco's premier ski resort.

Imlil and around

MAP OPPOSITE

You can take in the village of **Imlil** on a day-trip out of Marrakesh, 65km away, but it's more worthwhile if you spend a night or two there and do a bit of walking in the surrounding countryside. There's little to the village itself, which came into existence purely as a trekking base, and the only real sight, aside from the mountain scenery, is the *Kasbah du Toubkal*, formerly the palace of the local *caid* (chieftain), now a hotel and restaurant (see p.107 & p.83). To reach Imlil by public transport, get a shared *grand taxi* from the north end of Rue Oqba ben Nafaa to **Asni** (1hr; 20dh), where there are *grands taxis* on to Imlil (30min; 10dh). Occasionally there are taxis all the way for 30dh a seat. Alternatively, you could charter a *grand taxi* to take you up there from Marrakesh, which should work out at 400–450dh for the

Trekking in the High Atlas

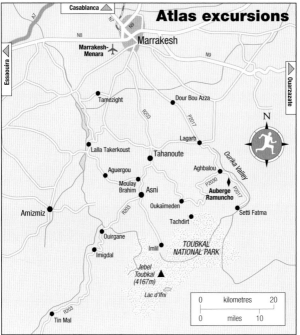

Atlas excursions

round trip, including three or four hours' waiting time.

From Imlil the mule trail back down to Asni is a relatively easy six-hour **hike**, and there are vehicles from Asni back to Marrakesh until around 5pm. Alternatively, you could just have **lunch** in Imlil and then head back into town by taxi.

You could also take on the short trek from Imlil to **Tachdirt** (3–4hr), which has a decent lodge in the centre of the village where you can spend the night. From Tachdirt, it's a day's trek down to **Setti Fatma** (see p.82), where there's transport back to Marrakesh.

With the right equipment, clothing and supplies, it's even possible to climb **Jebel Toubkal** (4167m), North Africa's highest peak, though this is not an ascent to be taken lightly.

Trekking and hiking in the Atlas

You could spend many days trekking in the High Atlas, but there are also trails to suit the casual hiker and routes that can be covered in a day. The easiest walks take in pretty valleys spread with a patchwork of little fields dotted with walnut trees.

To hire a **guide** (expect to pay around 500dh per day), contact the office (called *Bureau de Guides et Accompagnateurs en Montagne*) in Imlil (☎ 0524 485626, ⊛ bureaudesguidesimlil.com). In Marrakesh, the *Hotel Ali* (see p.96) is one of the best places to get **information** and arrange guides.

82

Setti Fatma and the Ourika Valley

MAP p.81

At the top of the highly scenic **Ourika Valley**, with high mountains and terraced fields on both sides, the village of **Setti Fatma**, 67km out of Marrakesh, is more picturesque than Imlil, and more worthwhile for a day-trip. The easiest way to get there is to take a shared *grand taxi* (a minibus in this case) from the southern end of Rue Oqba ben Nafaa (1hr; 20dh), or failing that, a shared taxi from Rue Ibn Rachid to **Lagarb** (also served by #25 bus from Place Youssef Tachfine), and another from there to Setti Fatma, or charter a whole taxi from Rue Ibn Rachid (400–450dh for the round-trip plus waiting time).

Setti Fatma is an excellent base for scenic **walks**, with six (sometimes seven) waterfalls above the village, the first of which can be reached very easily; you'll have no shortage of would-be guides offering to show you the way for a tip (of course), best agreed in advance. The walk to all seven falls and back takes around two and a half hours. If heading out for the falls in the morning, it's a good idea to order a tajine from one of the local restaurants (see opposite), which should be ready for when you get back.

Oukaïmeden

MAP p.81

The High Atlas village of **Oukaïmeden** ("Ouka" for short), 74km from Marrakesh, has five

Waterfalls at Setti Fatma

ski lifts and 20km of runs. There are nursery and intermediate runs on the lower slopes for the less advanced, and off-piste skiing and snowboarding are also available.

To get from Marrakesh to Oukaïmeden, you can charter a *grand taxi* for a day-trip (expect to pay 600dh there and back), or else get to Lagarb (see above), where there are minibuses to Oukaïmeden in season (Dec–April); coming back, try to leave by 3 or 4pm to be sure of transport connections.

Ski lift passes cost 110dh per day, and lessons are available from local instructors. You can rent **equipment** from shops near the hotel *Chez Juju* (see p.108) and at the bottom of the slope for around 120–150dh a day; snowboards and toboggans are also available.

Setti Fatma Moussem

Every year in mid-August, Setti Fatma holds a **moussem** dedicated to the local saint after whom the village is named. The saint's tomb stands by the river on the way to the waterfalls above the village. Although the moussem is religious in origin, it is just as much a fair and market, attracting Sufi mystics as well as performers like those of Marrakesh's Jemaa el Fna.

Restaurants: Imlil

Café Atlas Toubkal

300m up from the taxi stand and across the river ℹ 0676 047545. Daily 8am–8pm.

Perched on a rock with a rooftop terrace giving a vista over the village, this is a great place for a morning coffee, and pretty good for a tajine (80–90dh) at lunch.

Café les Amis

200m up the road from the taxi stand. Daily 9am–8pm.

Cheap and cheerful diner, with an upstairs terrace, which can lay on tajine for one, two or more if ordered at least an hour and a half in advance.

Kasbah du Toubkal

ℹ 0524 485611, ⓦ kasbahdutoubkal.com. Daily noon–3pm & 7–9.30pm.

This British-run hotel (see p.107) offers an excellent €30–35 (313–365dh) set menu, which should be booked at least a day in advance. In fact, the *Kasbah* can even organize the whole day-trip from Marrakesh as a package, at €85 (885dh) per person (minimum two). At the very least, it's worth popping in for a mint tea on their

Kasbah du Toubkal

scenic terrace. Unlicensed, but you can bring your own alcohol.

Maison Ait Mizane

150m up from the taxi stand ℹ 0652 159876. Daily 8am–10pm.

Tajines (15–35dh), soups, salads, juices and teas, served with a smile, in a little garden.

Restaurants: Ourika Valley

Hotel-Restaurant Asgaour

Setti Fatma, 200m below the taxi stand ℹ 0524 485294. Daily 7am–11pm.

One of the better choices among Setti Fatma's hotel restaurants, the *Asgaour* serves an excellent-value 50–55dh set menu, which you can eat inside, outside or across the river.

Hotel Setti Fatma

Setti Fatma, 300m below the taxi stand ℹ 0666 454972. Daily 7.30am–4pm.

The restaurant at this hotel (see p.108) is set in a garden overlooking the river, which makes it a lovely location for a meal. The set menu of salad, tagine and dessert is 120dh.

Restaurant Bouche de la Source

Setti Fatma, 100m above the taxi stand ℹ 0662 844694.

One of a group of small restaurants just across the river from the village (on a very rickety bridge), the *Bouche de la Source* has a series of scenic terraces and is a great place to stop for a meal (mains 60dh) or just a mint tea.

Restaurant le Noyer

Setti Fatma, 100m below the taxi stand ℹ 0661 596846. Daily 11am–4pm.

This restaurant with a riverside terrace offers a small selection of tasty tajines, brochettes and salads, with a choice of set menus (100–150dh).

Essaouira

Tourists have had a special relationship with the seaside resort of Essaouira, around 170km west of Marrakesh, since the 1960s, when its popularity as a hippy resort attracted the likes of Jimi Hendrix and Frank Zappa. Since then it has become a centre for artists and windsurfers, but despite increasing numbers of foreign visitors it remains one of the most laidback and likeable towns in Morocco. The whitewashed and blue-shuttered houses of its Medina, enclosed by spectacular ramparts, provide a colourful backdrop to a long, sandy beach, and whether you're here for the sport, the art or just the sand, you're sure to fall under its spell.

The Medina

MAP p.86, POCKET MAP E10–G12

The fairy-tale **ramparts** around Essaouira's Medina may look medieval, but they actually date from the reign of eighteenth-century sultan Sidi Mohammed Ben Abdallah, who commissioned a French military architect named Theodore Cornut to build a new town on a site previously occupied by a series of forts. The result is a walled medina that blends Moroccan and French layouts, combining a crisscross of main streets with a labyrinth of alleyways between them.

At the heart of the Medina are the main **souks**, centred on two arcades either side of Rue Mohammed Zerktouni. On the northwest side is the **spice souk**, where culinary aromatics join incense, traditional cosmetics and even natural aphrodisiacs billed as "herbal Viagra". Across the way, the **jewellers' souk** sells not just gems but also all kinds of crafts.

The western part of the Medina, the **Kasbah**, centres on **Place Prince Moulay el Hassan**. This is the town's main square, where locals and tourists alike linger over a mint tea or a coffee and enjoy the

Essaouira ramparts

The North Bastion

lazy pace of life. The square to the south, the **Mechouar**, is bounded by an imposing wall topped by a clocktower and flanked by palm trees, in whose shade townspeople often take a breather from the heat of the day.

The North Bastion

MAP p.86, POCKET MAP E10
Rue de la Skala. Daily sunrise–sunset. Free.

The city's **North Bastion** commands panoramic views across the Medina and out to sea.

It was one of the main Essaouira locations used in Orson Welles's 1952 screen version of *Othello*. Along the top is a collection of European **cannons**, presented to Sidi Mohammed Ben Abdallah by ambitious nineteenth-century merchants.

Down below, built into the ramparts along the Rue de la Skala, you can see some of the town's many **marquetry** and **woodcarving** workshops, where artisans produce amazingly painstaking and beautiful pieces from **thuya** wood.

Getting to Essaouira

Reaching Essaouira from Marrakesh by public transport is a cinch, though the journey time means you'll probably want to stay overnight. The cheapest way is to get a **bus** (19 daily; 3hr 30min; around 60dh) from the *gare routière* (see p.112). You arrive at Essaouira's *gare routière*, a ten-minute walk outside the town's Bab Doukkala, or a short *petit taxi* ride from the central Bab es Sebaa (7dh). A faster and more comfortable bus service is provided by **Supratours** (6 daily; 3hr; 75–100dh), leaving from their office in Marrakesh near the train station and arriving at Essaouira's Bab Marrakesh. **CTM**, the state bus company, also run two daily buses to Essaouira from the *gare routière* or from their office on Rue Abou Bakr Seddik (70dh). Finally, there are shared **grands taxis** to Essaouira (2hr 30min; 100dh) from the rank behind Marrakesh's *gare routière*; in Essaouira they might drop you in town itself, though they actually operate from a yard by the *gare routière*.

Essaouira's **airport**, 15km south of town, with no public transport (taxi 200dh for up to six) has flights to Luton with EasyJet. Essaouira's **tourist office** is located on Avenue du Caire (Mon–Fri 9am–4.30pm; ☎ 0524 783532).

Essaouira

ACCOMMODATION

Dar Adul	2
Dar al Bahar	1
Dar Ness	9
Hotel Beau Rivage	8
Hotel Cap Sim	5
Hotel Riad Al Medina	6
Hotel Souiri	7
Le Médina Essaouira Hotel	11
Riad Bab Essaouira	3
Riad Le Grand Large	4
Villa Maroc	10

North Bastion

Skala de la Ville
(woodworkers souk
below ramparts)

RUE OUM RABIA

RUE TOUAHEN

RUE DE LA SKALA

RUE BIN ROCHD

RUE LALLOU

PLACE
CHRIB
ATAI

AVENUE SIDI MOHAMM

KASBAH

R. KHALED BEN EL QUALD

R. SOUS

RUE EL
HAJALI

PL. PRINCE
MOULAY
EL HASSAN

RUE EL TETOUAN

RUE DE
MARRAKECH

RUE ATTARINE

PLACE
CHEFCHAOUNI

RUE DRIBE

MECHOUA

Clocktower

RUE ABDALLAH BEN HASSAN

AVENUE OKBA IBN NAFI

AVENUE DU CAIRE

Bab es Sebaa

PLACE
ORSON
WELLES

P

Fish
Grills

BOULEVARD MOHAMMED V

Marine Gate

Skala
du Port

Entrance
to port

Port

RESTAURANTS

Café-Restaurant Essalam	10
Café-Restaurant Laayoune	9
Chalet de la Plage	14
Dar Baba	5
Elizir	6
Fish Souk	1
La Maison du Cinéma	4
La Table by Madada	12
Les Alizes	3
Safran	2
Seafood grill stalls	13

BAR

Taros	1

CAFÉ

Café de France	8

PATISSERIES & ICE CREAM

Gelateria Dolce Freddo	11
Patisserie Driss	7

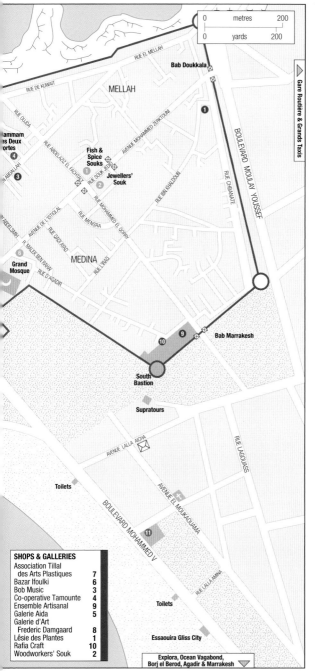

Gare Routière & Grands Taxis

0 metres 200
0 yards 200

RUE EL MELLAH

Bab Doukkala

MELLAH

RUE DE KUWAIT

RUE OUDIA

❶

BOULEVARD MOULAY YOUSSEF

Hammam
es Deux
ortes
❹

RUE ABDELAZIZ EL FACHTALI

RUE CHBANATE

IN ABDALLAH

❸

Fish &
Spice
Souks
❶

RUE SOUK JDID

Jewellers'
Souk
❷

AVENUE MOHAMMED ZERKTOUNI

RUE IBN KHALDOUNI

RUE MOHAMMED EL QORRY

RUE MENSRA

RUE ABDELSMIN

AVENUE DE L'ISTIQLAL

RUE QADI AYAD

R. MALEK BEN RAHAL

MEDINA

RUE URAQ

Grand
Mosque
❻

RUE D'AGADIR

Bab Marrakesh

❿ ❾

South
Bastion

Supratours

AVENUE LALLA AICHA

RUE LAGOUASS

Toilets

AVENUE EL MOUKAOUAMA

BOULEVARD MOHAMMED V

⓫

RUE LALLA AMINA

Toilets

Essaouira Gliss City

Explora, Ocean Vagabond,
Borj el Berod, Agadir & Marrakesh ▽

SHOPS & GALLERIES

Association Tillal des Arts Plastiques	7
Bazar Ifoulki	6
Bob Music	3
Co-operative Tamounte	4
Ensemble Artisanal	9
Galerie Aida	5
Galerie d'Art Frederic Damgaard	8
Lêsie des Plantes	1
Rafia Craft	10
Woodworkers' Souk	2

The Gnaoua Festival

Essaouira's main annual event is the **Gnaoua and World Music Festival** (Ⓦ festival-gnaoua.net), held in June. The festival focuses chiefly on the music of the Gnaoua, a Moroccan Sufi brotherhood with West African roots going back to the days of slavery. Stages are set up in the plaza between Place Prince Moulay el Hassan and the port, and outside Bab Marrakesh, and performers come from Morocco, Europe and West Africa. During the festival, you can expect hotels and transport to be full, so book well ahead if possible.

The Skala du Port

MAP p.86, POCKET MAP D12
Daily 9am–5pm. 10dh.

The **Skala du Port**, the square sea bastion by the harbour, is topped by lookout posts in each of its four corners and is worth popping into for the **views** from the ramparts. Looking east, you have a brilliant vista along the seaward side of the walled city. To the south, the Skala overlooks the bustling **port area**, where local wooden fishing boats are built or repaired, and where the fishing fleet brings in the day's catch.

Camel on Essaouira beach

The beach

MAP p.86, POCKET MAP E12

The main **beach**, to the south of town, extends for miles. On its closest stretches, the chief activity is **football** – a game is virtually always in progress, and at weekends there's a full-scale local league.

The wind here can be a bit remorseless for sunbathing in spring and summer, but it's perfect for **windsurfing**, and Essaouira is Morocco's number-one windsurfing resort. Surfing, windsurfing and kitesurfing equipment can be rented on the beach at Essaouira Gliss City (Ⓣ0661 343302, Ⓦessaouiraglisscity.com), 500m south of the Medina, where you can also arrange to have lessons. Equipment and lessons are also available 1km down the beach at Explora (Ⓣ0611 475188, Ⓦexploramorocco.com) or Ocean Vagabond (Ⓣ0524 783934, Ⓦoceanvagabond.com). The water is cool enough to make a wetsuit essential year-round.

If you head further along the beach, you'll pass the riverbed of the Oued Ksob (which can't be crossed at high tide) and come upon the ruins of an eighteenth-century circular fort, the **Borj el Berod**, which looks as though it is almost melting into the sand. The story that it inspired Jimi Hendrix's "Castles Made of Sand" is apocryphal, as the track was recorded before Hendrix came to Morocco.

Shops and galleries

Association Tillal des Arts Plastiques

MAP p.86, POCKET MAP E12
4 Av du Caire ☎ 0524 475424. Mon–Sat 9am–12.30pm & 3–7pm.

Essaouira's cheap and cheerful art gallery, where you can pick up small and affordable works of art by the fifty painters who make up this excellent local cooperative, including Najia Kerairate's colourful naive domestic scenes, and Hamid Bouhali's humorous caricatures of Moroccan life, for as little as 150dh.

Bazar Ifoulki

MAP p.86, POCKET MAP E11
1 Rue el Hajjali ☎ 0618 502440. Daily 10am–6pm.

This is a cheap and cheerful tailor's shop, where they make up a variety of light clothing in a choice of cotton or linen. Originally everything they made was in cream, white, black and grey: beautifully cool in Morocco's sometimes relentless heat. Nowadays they also sell clothes made of the same fabrics, but in a wider range of colours, some dark and sober, others bright and sunny. There are different sorts of shirts, drawstring-trousers, dresses and kaftans, at prices starting from 130dh.

Bob Music

MAP p.86, POCKET MAP F11
4 Rue Youssef Ben Tachfine ☎ 0668 252695. Daily 9am–8pm.

Named after Bob Marley, this musical instrument shop sells several types of Moroccan drums, Gnaoua castanets, lutes, *ginbris* (an instrument not unlike a lute, but rather more rustic), and even the sort of pipes used by snake charmers.

Co-operative Tamounte

MAP p.86, POCKET MAP E11
6 Rue Souss ☎ 0524 785611. Daily 9am–7pm.

This is a good place to buy both thuya marquetry and argan oil produced by cooperative enterprises. A co-op of fifteen artisans makes the thuya products, and a rural women's co-op makes the oil. In both cases, the quality is good and the prices are fixed, marked, and comparatively low, so you're not only contributing to fair-trade democratic enterprise, but also getting a good deal while you're at it.

Ensemble Artisanal

MAP p.86, POCKET MAP G12
Rue Mohammed el Qorry, just inside Bab Marrakesh. Daily 8am–6pm.

This bright, whitewashed courtyard hosts a handful of thuya carvers, an artisan jeweller – Mohammed Bizbiz, trained in Arab, Berber and Jewish styles – as well as a weaver, a leather shop, local artist Samad Sadiki (at the far end on the left) and inevitably, some marquetry workshops. In a courtyard on the right, a Brazilian ombú tree, one of only three in Morocco, was planted when the town was founded in the eighteenth century.

Ensemble Artisanal

Galerie Aida

MAP p.86, POCKET MAP E11
2 Rue de la Skala ☎ 0524 476290.
Daily 1–8pm.

Owned by a New Yorker, this shop starts off at the front selling secondhand books, mainly in English and at rather high prices, but as you head deeper inside, there's all kinds of interesting, superior bric-a-brac. Prices are still high, but at least you know you aren't getting sold any *trafika* (phoney antiques, unfortunately rather common in Essaouira's art and antique shops).

Galerie d'Art Frederic Damgaard

MAP p.86, POCKET MAP E12
Av Okba Ibn Nafi, Mechouar ☎ 0524 784446. Daily 9am–1pm & 3–7pm.

Essaouira's artists have made a name for themselves in both Morocco and Europe. Those whose paintings and sculptures are exhibited here in Essaouira's top gallery have developed their own highly distinctive styles, in some cases attracting an entourage of imitators. The gallery was founded by a Danish furniture

Galerie d'Art Frederic Damgaard

designer, and is now run by two Belgian art lovers, hand-picked by Damgaard to succeed him.

Lêsie des Plantes

MAP p.86, POCKET MAP G10
2 Rue Zaïr ☎ 0658 839397. Daily 7am–5pm.

The floor of this shop is covered with the shells of argan nuts, whose kernels are hulled and crushed (on the premises) to extract a much-prized nutty oil, which you can buy here, along with a wide range of culinary and medicinal herbs and spices, including excellent locally grown cumin and (when available) real Moroccan saffron. The proprietor is usually on hand to explain their various properties.

Rafia Craft

MAP p.86, POCKET MAP G12
82 Rue d'Agadir ☎ 0524 783632.
Mon–Sat 10am–1pm & 3–7pm.

A little-known local craft in Essaouira is the use of raffia (a strawlike fibre made from palm leaves) to make clothes, handbags, and above all, in this shop, shoes. All the items on sale here are the creations of local designer Miro Abihssira, and go for fixed prices, which are displayed at the counter. A pair of moccasins will set you back around 450dh for women's, 500dh for men's.

Woodworkers' souk

MAP p.86, POCKET MAP E10
Skala de la Ville, Rue de la Skala. Daily 8am–7pm, though individual shops vary.

The big buy in Essaouira is marquetry work made from thuya, an aromatic mahogany-like hardwood from a local coniferous tree, and the best place to buy it is this little souk, built into the ramparts of the Skala and dedicated to thuya marquetry. Artisans here produce amazingly painstaking and beautiful thuya work, which they justifiably claim is the best in the country.

Café

Café de France

MAP p.86, POCKET MAP E11
Pl Prince Moulay el Hassan. Daily
7am–10pm.

There's a feeling of faded French
imperialism to this 1917 colonial
café, still at the heart of Essaouira
street life a century on. In the
cavernous blue-and-white interior,
Souiris (the locals, that is) check
their betting slips over a *nuss-nuss*
(coffee half-and-half with milk)
while the tourists take their seats
outside on the square – Essaouira's
top people-watching spot by far.
The food's worth avoiding here,
but the coffee and the mint tea are
both excellent, and you couldn't
hope for a better location to linger
over them.

Patisseries and ice cream

Gelateria Dolce Freddo

MAP p.86, POCKET MAP E11
25 bis Pl Prince Moulay el Hassan
☏ 0663 571928. Daily 8am–10pm.

Delicious Italian ice creams at
just 15dh for a small (two-scoop)
cup or cone to take away, or 20dh
for a bowl to eat on the square.
The tiramisu flavour is heavenly,
the hazelnut isn't bad either, and
other flavours include forest fruits,
cherry ripple and lemon sorbet.

Patisserie Driss

MAP p.86, POCKET MAP E11
10 Rue el Hajali, just off Pl Prince Moulay
el Hassan ☏ 0524 475793. Daily 7am–9pm.

Serving delicious fresh pastries
and coffee in a quiet leafy
courtyard, this place is well
established (since 1928) as one of
Essaouira's most popular meeting
places. It's the ideal spot for a
leisurely breakfast (set breakfasts
26–32dh), or you can, of course,
buy pastries to go.

Gelateria Dolce Freddo

Restaurants

Café-Restaurant Essalam

MAP p.86, POCKET MAP E11
23 Pl Prince Moulay el Hassan. Daily
8am–noon & 7–11pm.

Essalam has some of the cheapest
set menus in town (30–70dh),
and certainly offers value for
money, with a choice of omelette,
tajine, fish, pastilla or couscous.
On the walls you will see small
watercolours by Brittany-born
Charles Kérival, who often visits
and paints in Essaouira.

Café-Restaurant Laayoune

MAP p.86, POCKET MAP E11
4 Rue el Hajali ☏ 0524 474643. Daily
noon–3pm & 6.45–10pm.

Laayoune is good for moderately
priced tajines and other Moroccan
staples in a relaxed setting with
friendly service, candlelit tables
and a menu in English on request.
You can eat à la carte (mains
50–78dh) or choose from a range
of tajine- and couscous-based set
menus (78–98dh).

Chalet de la Plage

MAP p.86, POCKET MAP E12
Bd Mohammed V, on the seafront, just
above the high-tide mark ☎ 0524 475972.
Daily noon–2.30pm & 6.30–10pm.

Originally built of wood by the
Ferraud family in 1924, the *Chalet
de la Plage* building, barnacled
with marine mementos, is now
a little gloomy, but the seafood
and sea views remain truly
memorable. Specialities include
sea bass steak, oyster tajine and
stuffed squid. Avoid lunchtime
when day-trippers overwhelm the
place. Licensed, with 180dh set
menus.

Dar Baba

MAP p.86, POCKET MAP E11
2 Rue de Marrakech ☎ 0524 476809.
Mon–Sat 7–10pm.

This upstairs restaurant has a
short but sweet menu of Italian
dishes, including mixed antipasti,
fish soup and (for dessert) sorbet.
It's most celebrated for its own
fresh pasta, though (50–75dh).
Licensed.

Elizir

MAP p.86, POCKET MAP F11
1 Rue d'Agadir ☎ 0524 472103. Daily
7.30–11pm.

This pioneering little restaurant
boasts eclectic retro decor and a
harmonious fusion of Italian and
Moroccan cuisine using locally
sourced ingredients. Dishes
change regularly but typically
include inky black cuttlefish
risotto, ricotta ravioli with basil
and pistachio and organic chicken
tajine with figs and gorgonzola.
Main courses go for 130–160dh.
Wine available.

Fish Souk

MAP p.86, POCKET MAP F11
Central souks (off Rue Souk Jedid).
Daily 9am–9pm.

For those in the know, this is the
place to get really fresh fish, better,
cheaper and minus the tricks and
hustle of the stalls by the port.

Taros

And it's nice and easy: you just
buy whatever wet fish you fancy –
anything from squid or sardine to
shark or swordfish – take it to the
restaurant in the southern corner
of the souk, and hey presto: for
30dh they'll cook it and serve it
straight up with fries and salad.
Yum yum.

La Maison du Cinema

MAP p.86, POCKET MAP E11
14 Rue Laâlouj ☎ 0524 784851,
ⓦ lamaisonducinema.net. Tues–Sun
8am–11pm.

A restaurant with a twist: as well
as dishing out tajines (50dh), they
show a different movie every night
at 8.30pm. Most of the films are in
French and a lot are dubbed, but
there's a good mix, and you can
watch for 90dh including a meal,
or 40dh including a drink.

La Table by Madada

MAP p.86, POCKET MAP E12
7 Rue Youssef el Fassi ☎ 0524 472106,
ⓦ www.latablemadada.com. Mon &
Wed–Sun noon–4pm & 7–10.30pm.

Housed in a former carob
warehouse, this restaurant offers
excellent, super-fresh seafood,

serving tapas at lunchtime, and full dinners in the evening, when they have wonderful fish dishes for 165dh, including monkfish kebabs, spider crab au gratin, sole or John Dory. Licensed.

Les Alizes

MAP p.86, POCKET MAP E11
28 Rue de la Skala ☏ 0524 476819.
Daily noon–3pm & 7–10pm.

This little place away from the mainstream has built itself quite a reputation for well-prepared traditional Moroccan dishes. Choice is limited to an 129dh set menu, but everything is absolutely delicious. Wine is available; booking advised.

Safran

MAP p.86, POCKET MAP F11
In the grain souk ☏ 0600 605031,
ⓦ lessaveursdusafran.com. Daily 8am–8pm.

A handy little budget restaurant, slap-bang in the middle of the Medina. They've got a variety of tajines, including camel and goat, or they can do you a fish couscous, should you so desire, but most people go for one of their set menus (75–120dh).

Grilled sardines, Essaouira style

Beverages include tea made with saffron instead of the usual spearmint, which is certainly worth a try.

Seafood grill stalls

MAP p.86, POCKET MAP E12
Off Pl Prince Moulay el Hassan, on the way to the port. Daily noon–10pm.

Very popular with visitors to Essaouira is a meal at one of these makeshift grill stalls, with wooden tables and benches. Each displays a selection of freshly caught fish, prawns, squid, lobster and other seafood delights – all you need to do is check the price (don't forget to do this or you'll be overcharged) and select the marine denizens of your choice, which are whisked off to the barbecue to reappear on your plate a few minutes later. Unfortunately, some of the stalls hustle shamelessly for business and (usually the same ones) may overcharge or pull stunts such as choosing you the most expensive fish – best policy is to avoid those that try to accost you. A plate of mixed fish with salad will set you back 60dh, a lobster or langouste supper about 150dh.

Bar

Taros

MAP p.86, POCKET MAP E11
Pl Moulay Hassan (entrance in Rue de la Skala) ☏ 0524 476407, ⓦ tarosessaouira .odns.fr. Daily 9am–midnight.

It's fun, fun, fun at this jolly rooftop bar with palm parasols and patio furniture, live music and even a house magician. It's the perfect spot to enjoy a beer or a cocktail around dusk, and the food's pretty good too, with dishes like fish and courgette lasagne, squid tajine or crab and spinach au gratin, for around 100–140dh a throw.

ACCOMMODATION

Riad Houdou

Accommodation

For many people, the main reason for coming to Marrakesh is to stay in a riad. These are stylish Medina guesthouses, mostly quite upmarket, and often very exclusive (see box, opposite). The Medina is also the place to find top-notch palatial hotels, such as *La Mamounia* and the *Maison Arabe*, as well as the widest range of mid-range hotels with character, usually in refurbished houses with en-suite rooms priced at 350–650dh. Most budget hotels are near the Jemaa el Fna, with double rooms for as little as 150–200dh a night, usually with shared bathrooms. Modern three-, four- and five-star hotels are concentrated in Guéliz and Hivernage; standards of service in the Hivernage package hotels are frankly amateurish, though they do offer wheelchair access, big pools and a child-friendly atmosphere. For more tranquil surroundings than you'll find in the city centre, it's worth considering hotels in Semlalia, at the northern end of the Ville Nouvelle, or better still, a place out in the Palmery to the northeast. Essaouira has a similar range of accommodation, including some lovely low-key riads, rather cheaper than those in Marrakesh, while sleeping options up in the Atlas mountains tend to be rougher and readier, mostly cheap little hotels and mountain refuges, though you can also stay in a former local chieftain's palace.

The Jemaa el Fna and the Koutoubia

HOTEL ADAY MAP p.28, POCKET MAP B12. 111 Derb Sidi Bouloukat ☎ 0524 441920, Ⓦ hotel-aday.com. This friendly budget hotel is well kept, clean and pleasantly decorated. Rooms with shared facilities are grouped around a central patio, and are small, with most having only inward-facing windows, but there's hot water round the clock, and also a newer wing with more comfortable, en-suite rooms. Alternatively, in summer, you can sleep on the roof for 40dh. Rates exclude breakfast. **154dh**

HOTEL AFRIQUIA MAP p.28, POCKET MAP B12. 45 Derb Sidi Bouloukat ☎ 0524 442403. This cheapo budget hotel, just off Rue Bab Agnaou, is extremely handy for the Jemaa el Fna, and when you've had enough of the hurly-burly, your bed's just a quick nip away. The rooms are simple but nice and airy, with shared bathrooms and rather hard beds; the ones on the top floor are the brightest. For lone travellers it also has single rooms at 80dh, which is about the cheapest in town. The attractive roof terrace is decorated Gaudí-style, with mosaics of broken tiles and crockery, but wi-fi reaches the lobby area only, and rates exclude breakfast. **150dh**

HOTEL ALI MAP p.28, POCKET MAP B12. Rue Moulay Ismail ☎ 0524 444979, Ⓦ hotel-ali.com. This busy hotel is used by groups heading to the High Atlas, so it's a good source of trekking (and other)

Riads

There are now hundreds of riads in Marrakesh, though they vary in quality, so it's worth shopping around. Literally, a "riad" means a patio garden, but the term has become synonymous with an upmarket guesthouse in a refurbished old mansion, whether it has a patio garden or not.

The trend started in the 1990s, when Europeans who'd bought houses in the Medina for their own use discovered they could make a pretty penny by taking in paying guests. Since then, the whole thing has escalated into something of an industry (a bubble waiting to burst in the eyes of some), and it's spread to other Moroccan cities, most notably Fez and Essaouira.

Riads range from plain and simple lodgings in a Moroccan family home (often called **maisons d'hôtes**, French for "guesthouse") to restored old mansions with classic decor. Many European-owned riads have been made up to look like something from an interior-design magazine, with swimming pools in the patio and jacuzzis on the roof. The best riads are stamped with the personality of the people who own them, often a couple or family who live alongside, and can be a good way to get a feel for Moroccan life.

Riad booking agencies

Marrakesh Medina 102 Rue Dar el Bacha, Northern Medina ☎ 0524 290707, ⓦ marrakech-medina.com. A firm that's actually in the business of doing up riads as well as renting them out, with a reasonable selection in all price ranges.

Marrakech Riads *Dar Cherifa*, 8 Derb Charfa Lakbir, Mouassine, Northern Medina ☎ 0524 426463, ⓦ marrakech-riads.net. A small agency with only nine riads; committed to keeping it chic and authentic.

information, and staff are always extremely helpful. They also change money, and can arrange car, minibus or 4WD rental, and there is free wi-fi. The place has a general air of business and being right in the middle of things, though that won't appeal to everyone. Rooms are en suite with a/c but very simple decor; they also vary in size, and some of them can get a bit whiffy in summer, so it's wise to check before taking one. Booking ahead is advisable. **€35 (380dh)**

HOTEL CENTRAL PALACE MAP p.28, POCKET MAP B12. 59 Derb Sidi Bouloukat ☎ 0524 440235. The rooms here are a cut above those in the other budget hotels in the back alleys south of the Jemaa el Fna, and correspondingly slightly pricier, but what this place also has going for it (aside from an in-house pizzeria and travel

agency) is its easy-to-find location, just off Rue Bab Agnaou, a stone's throw from the Jemaa. Rates exclusive of breakfast. **From 155dh**

HOTEL CTM MAP p.28, POCKET MAP B12. Jemaa el Fna ☎ 0524 442325. Right on the Jemaa el Fna in the heart of the action, the *Hotel CTM* is above the old bus station (hence its name), which is now used as a car park, so it's handy if you're driving. There are two categories of rooms: old and unmodernized with shared bathroom, or modernized and en suite with a/c in summer, heating in winter (250dh). The second category includes rooms 1–4, which overlook the square, giving you your own private view, though this does of course make them noisy. The roof terrace also overlooks the square. Breakfast excluded. **From 150dh**

Accommodation prices

Seasons vary slightly from establishment to establishment, but in general, **high season** for Marrakesh accommodation means March to May plus September and October; note that rates over the **Christmas/New Year** period can be as much as fifty percent higher than in the rest of the high season. The rates quoted here – which include **breakfast** unless otherwise stated – are for the cheapest double room in high season (excluding Christmas and New Year); the rest of the year, you can expect prices to be anything from ten to fifty percent cheaper. Most hotels fix their prices in dirhams, but some upmarket establishments fix them in euros or even pounds. For these places we've included the dirham price in brackets, and note that in all cases you'll be able to pay in local currency.

HOTEL DE FOUCAULD MAP p.28, POCKET MAP A13. Av el Mouahidine ☎ 0524 445499, ✉ hoteldefoucauld@gmail.com. Rooms are a little sombre and some are a bit on the small side, but they're decent enough, with a/c, heating and constant hot water (with a choice of tub or shower). There's a roof terrace with views of the Koutoubia, and a restaurant with buffet suppers. The staff can arrange tours, help with local information and put you onto guides for High Atlas trekking. Excludes breakfast. **295dh**

HOTEL GALLIA MAP p.28, POCKET MAP B13. 30 Rue de la Recette ☎ 0524 445913, ✉ hotelgallia.com. A beautifully kept hotel in a restored Medina mansion, the *Gallia* has immaculate en-suite rooms off two tiled courtyards, one with a fountain, palm tree and caged birds. There's central heating in winter and a/c in summer. It's a long-time favourite and highly recommended. Book online, at least a month ahead if possible. Rates exclude breakfast. **460dh**

HOTEL ICHBILIA MAP p.28, POCKET MAP B12. 1 Rue Bani Marine ☎ 0524 381530. Near the Cinéma Mabrouka, and well placed for shops, banks and cafés, the *Ichbilia* has rooms off a covered gallery. Some are plain and simple, but still clean and comfortable, others have a/c and private bathrooms. Some locals will know it as the *Hotel Sevilla*, Ichbilia being the Arabic for Seville. Rates exclude breakfast. **180–320dh**

HOTEL LA MAMOUNIA MAP p.28, POCKET MAP E6. Av Bab Jedid ☎ 0524 388600, ✇ mamounia.com. Set in palatial grounds, this is Marrakesh's most famous hotel, and its most expensive, with an emphasis on opulence and exclusivity. Decoratively, it is of most interest for the 1920s Art Deco touches by Jacques Majorelle (of Majorelle Garden fame), and their enhancements, in 1986, by the then Moroccan king's favourite designer, André Paccard. The rooms are done out in warm reds and browns, with magnificent marble bathrooms, but some of the simple "classic" rooms can be on the small side, so it's best to pay a bit more for a "superior" or "deluxe" (and there's a range of suites and riads costing up to ten times more). *La Maison Arabe* (see p.100) is generally better value if you're looking to be pampered, but it can't match the *Mamounia*'s facilities or architectural splendour. Standard doubles (excluding breakfast) cost **7500dh**

HOTEL MEDINA MAP p.28, POCKET MAP B12. 1 Derb Sidi Bouloukat ☎ 0524 442997, ✇ hotelmedinamarrakech.com. Located in a street full of good budget hotels, the *Medina* is a perennial favourite among the cheapies, and often full. It's clean, friendly and pretty good value, and there's always hot water in the shared showers. The owner – who used to work in Britain as a circus acrobat – speaks good English. They have a small roof terrace and in summer there's also the option of sleeping on the roof (40dh). **150dh**

HOTEL SHERAZADE MAP p.28, POCKET MAP B12. 3 Derb Djama, off Rue Riad Zitoun el Kadim Ⓣ 0524 429305, Ⓦ hotelsherazade.com. This old merchant's house, attractively done up, was already on the scene before riads took off big time. Besides a lovely roof terrace, the hotel offers a wide variety of well-maintained rooms in pretty pastel colours, not all en suite. Run very professionally by a German-Moroccan couple, it's extremely popular, so book well ahead. Rates exclude breakfast. **From 230dh**

JNANE MOGADOR HOTEL MAP p.28, POCKET MAP B12. Derb Sidi Bouloukat, by 116 Rue Riad Zitoun el Kadim Ⓣ 0524 426324, Ⓦ jnanemogador.com. This upmarket yet homey hostelry has established itself as a favourite among Marrakesh's mid-range accommodation. Set in a beautifully restored old house, it boasts charming rooms, in warm tints with modern furnishings, around a lovely fountain patio, with its own hammam and a roof terrace where you can have breakfast, or tea and cake. **480dh**

RIAD ZINOUN MAP p.28, POCKET MAP C13. 31 Derb Ben Amrane, off Rue Riad Zitoun el Kadim Ⓣ 0524 426793, Ⓦ riadzinoun. com. A friendly little riad, run by a French-Moroccan couple, the *Zinoun* isn't the most chic of its kind in the Medina, but this nicely refurbished old house is agreeably relaxing, with a pleasant central patio (covered in winter, open in summer), and rooms decorated with rugs and traditional painted-wood furniture. **From €54 (570dh)**

The Northern Medina

DAR EL ASSAFIR MAP p.38, POCKET MAP E4. 24bis Arset el Hamed Ⓣ 0524 387377, Ⓔ darelassafir@gmail.com, Ⓦ facebook.com/pg/RiadDarElAssafir. Located behind the town hall, in a part of the Medina open to traffic, this is a late nineteenth-century colonial mansion decorated in colonial rather than traditional style. It's quite spacious, with two patios and a nice pool, singing birds in a little aviary and belle époque-style rooms with oriental-style ornaments. **From €90 (980dh)**

DAR IHSSANE MAP p.38, POCKET MAP B11. 14 Derb Chorfa el Kebir, near Mouassine Mosque Ⓣ 0524 387826, Ⓦ dar-ihssane. com. *Dar Ihssane* is a good-value riad in a mansion which dates back to at least the seventeenth or eighteenth century, and possibly even to the Middle Ages (it has two medieval pillars, discovered during renovation, which may be part of an original building, or recycled from elsewhere). The rooms are small, but light and airy. It's owned by the nephew of painter Georges Bretegnier, and is decorated with some of Bretegnier's original paintings and drawings. **From 385dh**

DAR MOUASSINE MAP p.38, POCKET MAP A11. 148 Derb Essnane, off Rue Sidi el Yamami Ⓣ 0524 445287, Ⓦ darmouassine.com. The rooms here have classic Moroccan decor, the salon and the patio (which also has a fountain and banana trees) less so. There are well-chosen and interesting prints on the walls, all rooms have audio players, and the better ones have painted wooden ceilings. **From €105 (1100dh)**

DAR SALAM MAP p.38, POCKET MAP F3. 162 Derb Ben Fayda, off Rue el Gza near Bab Moussoufa Ⓣ 0524 384141, Ⓔ rayadsalam@yahoo.fr. This is a true *maison d'hôte* as opposed to a riad: a Moroccan family home that takes in guests, and a place to relax and put your feet up rather than admire the decor. The food is similarly unpretentious – tasty home-style Moroccan cooking, like your mum would make if she were Marrakshi. **From €40 (430dh)**

EL FENN MAP p.38, POCKET MAP A12. 2 Derb Moulay Abdellah Ben Hessaien, Bab el Ksour Ⓣ 0524 441210, Ⓦ el-fenn. com. This super-deluxe boutique hotel was set up by artist and art dealer Vanessa Branson, and has its own art gallery. An innovative mix of classic and modern, it's spacious and super-stylish, with a mix of different rooms and suites, great service and six pools (three of them private), and a roof terrace with great Koutoubia views. The annexe is less swish than the main hotel, however, and oddly, they don't take cash here, so bring your flexible friend. **From €350 (3800dh)**

EQUITY POINT MARRAKECH MAP p.38. POCKET MAP B11. 80 Derb el Hammam Mouassine ☏ 0524 440793, ⓦ equity-point.com. A hostel in a riad, with all the architectural charm of any other riad, but a fun crowd and four- to eight-bed dorms instead of the usual flowers-on-the-pillow service. There's wi-fi, a pool, a bar and a restaurant, cool spaces to hang out in, and a friendly atmosphere. Breakfast not included. Dorms €15.90 (170dh), doubles from €55 (580dh)

LA MAISON ARABE MAP p.38, POCKET MAP E4. 1 Derb Assehbi Bab Doukkala, behind the Doukkala Mosque ☏ 0524 387010, ⓦ lamaisonarabe.com. Though not as famous as the *Mamounia*, this is arguably Marrakesh's classiest hotel, a gorgeous nineteenth-century mansion that's been restored with fine traditional workmanship. The furnishings are classic Moroccan and sumptuous, as is the food (it even offers cookery classes), and standards of service are high. There are two beautifully kept patios and a selection of rooms and suites, all in warm colours with comfortable modern furnishings, some with private terrace and jacuzzi. There is no pool on the premises, but a free shuttle bus can take you to the hotel's private pool nearby. Rates include afternoon tea as well as breakfast. From 2500dh

NOIR D'IVOIRE MAP p.38, POCKET MAP F4. 31 Derb Jedid, Bab Doukkala ☏ 0524 380975, ⓦ noir-d-ivoire.com. This magnificent riad is impressive from the moment you walk in. It's owned by an English interior designer, who's decorated it in cream, brown and black (the name refers to the colour scheme), with a feel that manages to be both classic and modern, classy yet cosy, all at the same time. There's a well-equipped gym, two pools and a bar, and service is punctilious, reflecting the fact that there's almost one staff member per guest. From 2362dh

RIAD 72 MAP p.38, POCKET MAP F4. 72 Derb Arset Aouzal ☏ 0524 387629, ⓦ riad72.com. This Italian-owned riad is sleek and stylish, with sparse but very tasteful modern decor, palms and banana trees in the courtyard and its own hammam (but no pool). The catering is Moroccan. It's part of a group called Uovo (Italian for "egg") who have a similarly stylish sister establishment, *Riad Due* at 2 Derb Chentouf (ⓦ riaddue. com). Rates include breakfast, afternoon tea and one airport transfer. From €173 (1820dh)

RIAD AL MASSARAH MAP p.38, POCKET MAP E4. 26 Derb Jedid, Bab Doukkala ☏ 0524 383206, ⓦ riadalmassarah.com. Light defines this cool, airy riad. It's done out in white, and rather minimalist, but for all that it's small, friendly and quite intimate, and the owners (one French, one British) are great hosts. There's solar-heated water, a pool and a real fire in most rooms. The riad encourages responsible tourism and supports local charities. Rates include breakfast and afternoon tea. From 1246dh

RIAD CAMILIA MAP p.38, POCKET MAP C10. 9 Derb el Ouali, Kaat Benahid ☏ 0524 443081, ⓦ riadcamilia.com. Made out of four old houses with three patios (one of which is private to one of the suites), this is a riad whose landlord lives in, giving it the personal touch that a good riad really needs. Although it isn't easy to find (hidden down a tunnel-like passage), it's actually very handy for the souks and for the sights around Place Ben Youssef. It's got a great roof terrace, where a lot of the herbs they use in the kitchen are grown (mint, rosemary, lemongrass, wormwood), and the decor is tasteful and refined. From €130 (1400dh)

RIAD DANKA MAP p.38, POCKET MAP C11. 141 Derb Aarjane (off Pl Rahba Kedima) ☏ 0524 440404, ⓦ riaddanka. com. This elegant little riad has just six rooms, and the owners are usually on hand to look after their guests in person. The decor is restrained but attractive, in black, white and earth colours, there's a large pool downstairs (heated in winter) and a smaller one on the roof, in case you need a dip to cool down in summer. And, in contrast to many riads, the in-house hammam is free for guests and open all day to use when you want. €120 (1290dh)

RIAD FARNATCHI MAP p.38, POCKET MAP C10. 2 Derb el Farnatchi, off Rue Bin Lafnadek ☏ 0524 384910, Ⓦ www.riadfarnatchi.com. The suites (there are no ordinary rooms) at this efficient and professionally run British-owned riad are spacious, each with either a balcony, a private terrace or its own patio, though the understated decor incorporates some quite rustic features. There are also two common patios, one with a pool, and the salons and dining rooms are very stylish. Rates include breakfast, free airport transfer, free hot and cold drinks, and canapés before dinner. **From 3400dh**

RIAD HOUDOU MAP p.38, POCKET MAP H4. 54 Derb el Hammam Issebtyine, El Moukef ☏ 0524 383793, Ⓦ riadhoudou.com. A small riad in a seventeenth-century house, whose English-speaking French owners live in, giving the place a very personal touch, and also means they are on hand to dispense advice and recommendations. Decor is classic with light-hearted modern touches (purple iron cacti on the roof terrace, for example), and pets include tortoises, a cat and a chameleon. **Rooms start at €69 (750dh)**

RIAD KHEIRREDINE MAP p.38, POCKET MAP F3. 2 Derb Chelligui, Sidi Ben Slimane ☏ 0524 386364, Ⓦ riadkheirredine.com. Super-cool and very welcoming Italian-run riad (although most of the guests are from English-speaking countries), with two patios and two pools, rooms and public spaces done out in delicious creams and dark chocolate browns, in a residential part of the Medina, very handy for the Majorelle Garden and the bus station. The staff go out of their way to be as helpful as possible. **From €160 (1700dh)**

RIAD KNIZA MAP p.38, POCKET MAP E4. 34 Derb l'Hotel, near Bab Doukkala ☏ 0524 376942, Ⓦ riadkniza.com. Owned by a top antique dealer and tour guide (whose clients have included US presidents and film stars), this is one classy riad. The rooms are beautiful, with classic Moroccan decor, and there's a state-of-the-art pool,

not to mention a sauna, hammam and massage room, real antiques for decoration, and solar panels for ecologically sound hot water – yet it still manages to feel like a real Moroccan family home. The family themselves (all English-speaking) are always available to make you feel welcome, the food is excellent and the service is absolutely impeccable. **From €210 (2210dh)**

RIAD LES TROIS PALMIERS MAP p.38, POCKET MAP A10. 36 Derb Tizougarine, near Dar el Bacha ☏ 0600 024560, Ⓦ riadlestroispalmiers.com. Two adjoining eighteenth-century mansions, originally built for two branches of the same family, have now been reunited to make this graceful riad. The decor is predominantly brown and cream, with lots of original features including a lovely painted ceiling, and the three palms that give the riad its name, which grow in one of the two patios. Under French ownership though English is spoken too. Prices include breakfast. **From €160 (1665dh)**

RIAD MALIKA MAP p.38, POCKET MAP F4. 29–36 Derb Arset Aouzal ☏ 0524 385451, Ⓦ riadmalika.com. Sumptuous decor – modern but with colonial and 1930s touches – bedecks this very stylish riad owned by architect and interior designer Jean-Luc Lemée. There's loads of chequered tiling, a lovely pool, a warm salon and plush bedroom furnishings. It's very popular and needs booking well ahead. **From €100 (1050dh)**

RIAD PAPILLON MAP p.38, POCKET MAP B10. 15 Derb Tizougarine, near Dar el Bacha ☏ 0614 234965, reservations UK ☏ +44 20 7570 0336, US ☏ +1 800 845 0810, Ⓦ riadpapillon.com. The staff go out of their way to help you feel at home in this small but very friendly riad. They also keep the place scented with jasmine oil, which you may or may not like. The rooms are named after flowers, but rather than being frilly are sparsely yet tastefully decorated with small touches. The same firm also run the *Henna Café* (see p.48) and *Riad Star* (see p.102). **From £100 (1240dh)**

RIAD ROMANCE MAP p.38, POCKET MAP H3. 26 Derb el Baroud, Hart Essoura ☎ 0524 387606, ⓦ riadromance.com. Nice for a bit of romance, but welcoming to single travellers and non-couples too, this little riad has a spacious main patio with (for a riad) a large pool, a small roof terrace, and a light, modern feel, with classic touches (the building is seventeenth-century). The English-speaking owners don't live in, but are usually on hand to look after guests and dispense knowledge and information. From €119 (1300dh).

RIAD SAFA MAP p.38, POCKET MAP H4. 64 Derb Lalla Azouna, off Rue Essebtiyne ☎ 0524 377123, ⓦ riad-safa.com. There's a sun-bleached look to this small, rather unassuming, rustic-feeling riad, with lots of whitewash and unvarnished wood, plus a few sparse splashes of colour. It's also quite intimate, with only five rooms and two patios. There's also a roof terrace complete with jacuzzi and of course an in-house hammam. From €75 (790dh).

RIAD SAHARA NOUR MAP p.38, POCKET MAP E4. 118 Derb Dekkak ☎ 0524 376570, ⓦ riadsaharanour-marrakech.com. More than just a riad, this is a centre for art, self-development and relaxation. Art workshops in music, dance, painting and calligraphy are held here, and self-development programmes in meditation and relaxation techniques are available. Guests who wish to hold artistic happenings are encouraged, but you don't need to take part in these activities in order to stay here and enjoy the calm atmosphere on the patio, shaded by orange, loquat and pomegranate trees. From €75 (790dh).

RIAD STAR MAP p.38, POCKET MAP C10. 31 Derb Alailich (off Rue de Souk des Fassis) ☎ 0656 566374, UK ☎ +44(0)20 7570 0336, USA ☎ +1 800 845 0810, ⓦ riadstar.com. Run by the same people as *Riad Papillon* (see p.101) and the *Henna Café* (see p.48), this is the former home of jazz dancer Josephine Baker, who lived here during World War II, when she was a spy for Free France. The riad is themed on her era, with memorabilia and even costumes that you can wear. The rooms are stylish, with black-tiled bathrooms and there's an in-house hammam and a rooftop sun terrace. From £112 (1375dh).

Hammams

Even the cheapest hotels in Marrakesh have bathroom facilities, sometimes shared, but for a really Moroccan bathing experience, it's worth trying a hammam.

A hammam is a Turkish-style **steam bath**, with a succession of rooms ranging in temperature from cool to hot, and endless supplies of hot and cold water, which you fetch in buckets. The usual procedure is to find a piece of floor space in the hot room, surround it with as many buckets of water as you feel you need, and lie in the heat to sweat out the dirt from your pores before scrubbing it off. A plastic bowl is useful for scooping the water from the buckets to wash with. You can also order a **massage**, in which you will be allowed to sweat, pulled about a bit to relax your muscles, and then rigorously scrubbed with a rough flannel glove (*kiis*). Alternatively, buy a *kiis* and do it yourself. Note that complete **nudity** is taboo, so you should keep your underwear on (bring a dry change) or wear a swimming costume, and change with a towel around you.

For many Moroccan **women**, who would not go out to a café or bar, the hammam is a social gathering place, in which women tourists are made very welcome too. Indeed, hammams turn out to be a highlight for many women travellers, and an excellent way to make contact with Moroccan women.

RIAD ZOLAH MAP p.38, POCKET MAP B11. 114–116 Derb el Hammam, near Mouassine Mosque ☎0524 387535, ⓦ riadzolah.com. An English-owned riad run with flair by a vivacious English-speaking Moroccan manager, this is really a lovely place to stay. You get a free pair of Moroccan slippers when you arrive, fresh and dried fruit in your room daily and all sorts of little touches that make you feel like a special guest ("the most generous range of extras in Marrakesh", so they claim). Facilities include wi-fi, in-house hammam and massage room, and the decor is tasteful with lots of white, big splashes of colour, original features and wonderful use of carpets and drapes. Rates include breakfast and airport transfers. **From €107 (1115dh)**

RIYAD EL CADI MAP p.38, POCKET MAP C11. 86–87 Derb Moulay Abdelkader, off Rue Dabachi ☎ 0524 378098, ⓦ riyadelcadi.com. The former home of a German diplomat who was ambassador to several Arab countries, the *El Cadi* is embellished with his wonderful collection of rugs and antiques. It incorporates five patios, three salons, a pool, a hammam,

and excellent standards of service. The rooms vary in style, each having a theme (camels in the Camel Room, for example) on which the decor is based, and as well as ordinary guest rooms, there are two wonderful suites, and the "blue house", a patio with two double rooms, which is rented in its entirety. **From €140 (1540dh)**

The Southern Medina and Agdal Gardens

DAR LES CIGOGNES MAP p.54, POCKET MAP H7. 108 Rue Berrima ☎ 0524 382740, ⓦ lescigognes.com. This luxury boutique hotel, run by a Swiss–American couple, gets consistently good reports. It takes the form of two converted Medina houses done up in traditional fashion around the patio, but with modern decor in the rooms and suites. Features include a library, a hammam, a jacuzzi, a salon and a terrace where you can see storks nesting on the walls of the royal palace opposite (hence the name, which means "house of the storks"), and cookery lessons are available. All rooms are en suite. **From 1282dh**

There are quite a lot of hammams in the Medina; the three closest to the Jemaa el Fna (all south of the square) are **Hammam Polo** on Rue de la Recette; **Hammam Sidi Bouloukate**, just round the corner from *Hotel Central Palace*; and one (unsigned) at the northern end of Rue Riad Zitoun el Kadim. All three are open from 6am to 8pm for women and the same or slightly longer for men, with separate entrances for each sex, and all cost 12dh. Don't forget to bring along some soap and shampoo (though these are often sold at the hammam), and a towel (these are sometimes rented, but can be a bit dubious).

In addition to ordinary Moroccan hammams, there are also upmarket tourist hammams such as **Hammam Ziani**, 14 Rue Riad Zitoun el Jedid (☎ 0662 715571, ⓦ www.hammamziani.ma; daily 7am–10pm), open for both sexes (separate areas), costing 50dh for a simple steam bath, or 350dh for an all-in package with massage. Even posher is **Les Bains de Marrakech**, 2 Derb Sedra, down an alley by Bab Agnaou in the Kasbah (☎ 0524 386419, ⓦ lesbainsdemarrakech.com; daily 9am–7.30pm), where prices start at 200dh and you'll need to book in advance. Despite these high prices, you won't (unless you're gay) be able to share a steam bath experience with your partner – if you want to do that, you'll have to stay at one of the many riads listed in this chapter with their own in-house hammam.

LA SULTANA MAP p.54, POCKET MAP G7. 403 Rue de la Kasbah ☏ 0524 388008, Ⓦ lasultanamarrakech.com. For those who can't decide between a riad, a five-star or a boutique hotel, this is an extremely stylish blend of all three: riad style, boutique personal attention and five-star amenities. Facilities include a hammam, pool, jacuzzi, spa, lounge bar, library, panoramic terraces and excellent dining – all just round the corner from Bab Agnaou and the Saadian Tombs. Rates exclude breakfast. **From 4700dh**

LE CLOS DES ARTS MAP p.54, POCKET MAP C13. 50 Derb Tbib, off Rue Riad Zitoun el Jedid ☏ 0524 375159, Ⓦ leclosdesarts. com. This beautiful riad is filled with the works of one of the proprietors, who is a painter and sculptor as well as an interior designer. Each room has its own style and colour, and the whole effect is warm and delightful, as are the owners, who give it a real personal touch. Workshops on Moroccan art techniques are available. **€160 (1665dh)**

LES JARDINS DE LA MEDINA MAP p.54, POCKET MAP G9. 21 Derb Chtouka, Kasbah ☏ 0524 381851, Ⓦ lesjardinsdelamedina. com. This beautiful old palace has been transformed into a truly sumptuous hotel. The 36 rooms, each with its own character and individual decor, are set around an extensive patio garden with hammocks slung between the trees and a decent-sized pool. What the hotel really plugs, however, is its hammam-cum-beauty salon where you can get manicured, pedicured, scrubbed and massaged till you glow. **From €264 (2750dh)**

RIAD & SPA BAHIA SALAM MAP p.54, POCKET MAP G7. 61 Av Houmane el Fetouaki ☏ 0524 426060, Ⓦ riadbahiasalam.com. Despite its name, this converted nineteenth-century mansion, decorated in Marrakesh red ochre with lots of zellij and carved cedar, is really a good-value and quite stylish hotel rather than a riad. Its main attraction is its full range of hammam and spa facilities, though the rooms are modern and elegant. It's also very centrally located, with parking directly across the street. **From €70 (730dh)**

RIAD AGUERZAME MAP p.54, POCKET MAP H6. 66 Derb Jedid, Douar Graoua ☏ 0524 381184, Ⓦ riadaguerzame. com. A small, intimate riad – only four rooms – with a personal touch supplied by its genial, English-speaking Breton host, who's invariably on hand to look after you, and dispense local advice and information about the neighbourhood. **€99 (1080dh)**

RIAD AKKA MAP p.54, POCKET MAP H6. 65 Derb Lahbib Magni, off Rue de la Bahia ☏ 0524 375767, Ⓦ riad-akka -marrakech.com. Orange, grey and black decor characterize the public areas of this stylish, modern riad, where all of the furniture was designed by one of the French owners and there's a different colour scheme for every room. It's particularly favoured by golfing enthusiasts, but pleasing to anyone with a sense of style. **From €120 (1250dh)**

RIAD BAYTI MAP p.54, POCKET MAP H7. 35 Derb Saka, Bab el Mellah ☏ 0524 380180, Ⓦ riad-bayti.com. The high ceilings and wide veranda typical of old Mellah houses give a spacious feel to this riad, formerly owned by a family of Jewish wine merchants. It's run by a dynamic young French couple, and its warm modern decor perfectly complements the classic architecture and the smell of spices wafting in from the market below. Facilities include free childcare and wi-fi. Rates include breakfast and afternoon tea. **From €80 (830dh)**

RIAD DAR ONE MAP p.54, POCKET MAP H7. 19 Derb Jemaa el Kebir, Mellah ☏ 0600 021381, Ⓦ riad-dar-one.com. This old Mellah house has been renovated in quite minimalist modern style, with beige, brown and white decor, and lashings of tadelakt (see p.127). It's very handy for sights like the Bahia and El Badi palaces, and the staff are invariably usually around to make you feel at home and give help and advice. From €90 (935dh)

RIYAD AL MOUSSIKA MAP p.54, POCKET MAP C12. 62 Derb Boutouil, Kennaria ☏ 0524 389067, Ⓦ riyad-al-moussika. com. This gem of a riad was once owned by French former governor, Thami el Glaoui. A harmonious and beautiful combination of Moroccan tradition and Italian flair, its decor is gorgeous – like a traditional Marrakshi mansion, but better. The walls are decked with local art, and the Italian owner's son, a cordon bleu chef, takes care of the catering – in fact, the riad claims to have the finest cuisine in town. Rate includes breakfast, lunch and afternoon tea. **€150 (1560dh)**

VILLA DES ORANGERS MAP p.54, POCKET MAP F7. 6 Rue Sidi Mimoun, off Pl Youssef Ben Tachfine ☎ 0524 384638, ⓦ villadesorangers.com. Officially classified as a hotel, this place is in fact a riad in the true sense of the term: an old house around a patio garden (three gardens in fact), with orange trees and a complete overdose of lovely carved stucco. There's a range of rooms and suites – many with their own private terrace – as well as three pools (one on the roof), two restaurants and a spacious salon with a real fireplace. A light lunch, as well as breakfast, is included in the price. **From 6702dh**

The Ville Nouvelle and Palmery

DAR ZEMORA MAP p.65, POCKET MAP J1. 72 Rue el Aandalib, Palmery, 3km from town ☎ 0524 328200, reservations UK ☎ +44 20 7583 9265, ⓦ darzemora.com. This British-owned luxury villa, stylishly embellished with a mix of traditional and modern features, has a pleasant garden with a pool, a masseur on call and a view of the Atlas mountains from the roof terrace. All rooms have CD players though no TV. To find it, take the next left (Rue Qortoba) off the Route de Fès after the Circuit de la Palmeraie, then the first right (Rue el Yassamin), fork left after 300m and it's 300m round the bend on the right. Breakfast and afternoon tea included. **£215 (2540dh)**

GRAND MOGADOR MENARA MAP p.65, POCKET MAP B6. Av Mohammed VI (Av de France), Hivernage ☎ 0524 339330, ⓦ mogadorhotels.com. The facilities at this five-star hotel (though it's really more like a four-star) include a health club and three restaurants. The lobby is decorated in classic style, with painted ceilings, chandeliers and a very Moroccan feel, and the receptionists wear traditional garb. Rooms, on the other hand, are modern, light and airy. There's also a pool. **2200dh**

HOTEL ATLAS MEDINA MAP p.65, POCKET MAP B6. Av Moulay el Hassan, Hivernage ☎ 0524 339999, ⓦ atlas5stars.com. Set amid extensive gardens planted with no fewer than two hundred palm trees, this is the Atlas chain's top offering in Marrakesh. It's best known for its spa facilities, which offer treatments using traditional Moroccan hammam cosmetics such as *ghassoul* mud-shampoo, here used for a facial rather than to wash hair. Rooms are modern and carpeted, with cosy red and orange decor. Breakfast excluded. **From €75 (780dh)**

HOTEL DU PACHA MAP p.65, POCKET MAP B14. 33 Rue de la Liberté, Guéliz ☎ 0524 431327, ⓦ hotelpacha.net. Built in the 1930s, this colonial-era hotel promises to offer a journey back in time, and pretty much does; it's sedate, slightly drab, but friendly and homely, and very much a respectable old-school Moroccan hotel. The rooms are modernized, with a/c and modern bathrooms, and some have balconies. **From 440dh**

HOTEL FAROUK MAP p.65, POCKET MAP B15. 66 Av Hassan II, Guéliz ☎ 0524 431989, ⓦ hotelfarouk.com. Housed in a rather eccentric building, with all sorts of extensions, the *Farouk* offers a variety of rooms – have a look at a few before choosing – all with hot showers. Staff are friendly and there's an excellent restaurant. Owned by the same family as the *Ali* in the Medina. Prices exclusive of breakfast. **210dh**

HOTEL FASHION MAP p.65, POCKET MAP B15. 45 Av Hassan II, Guéliz ☎ 0524 423707, ✉ fashionhotel@hotmail.fr, ⓦ hotelfashionmarrakech.com. Terracotta tiling, nicely carved black-painted wooden furnishings and large windows grace the rooms at this tastefully designed three-star, where the bathrooms feature reliable hot showers with a strong jet. There's also a rooftop pool and basement hammam. **550dh**

HOTEL TAFOUKT MAP p.65, POCKET MAP A2. 116 Place du Petit Marché, off Route de Targa, Guéliz ☎ 0524 379000, ⓦ hoteltafouktmarrakech.com. This small hotel is a definite cut above most of the Ville Nouvelle options, and great value for money. All the rooms are "junior suites" (that is, they have a sitting area as well as a bedroom area, but not as separate rooms), and the place is well-kept and has room service, a spa and a pool. It isn't as grand as a five-star, but it's a lot more personal; it doesn't call itself a "boutique hotel", but that's basically what it is. **From 750dh**

HOTEL TICHKA MAP p.65, POCKET MAP A1. Off Bd Mohammed Abdelkrim el Khattabi, Semlalia, about 1km north of the junction with Av Mohammed V (served by bus #1 from the Koutoubia) ☎ 0524 448710, ⓦ hotel-marrakech-tichka.com. Built in 1986, this hotel boasts decor by Tunisian architect Charles Boccara and American interior designer Bill Willis, including columns in the form of stylized palm trees reminiscent of ancient Egypt. Willis's use here of tadelakt (see p.127) made it massively trendy in Moroccan interior design (most riads use lots of it). Rooms are modern and cosy, in brown and cream, and the hotel has a swimming pool, a health centre and its own hammam, and one room is adapted for wheelchair users. The staff are friendly but the hotel is getting a bit worn around the edges. Big discounts often available online. **2033dh, excluding breakfast**

HOTEL TOULOUSAIN MAP p.65, POCKET MAP B14. 44 Rue Tarik Ben Ziad, Guéliz ☎ 0524 430033, ⓦ hoteltoulousain.ma. This excellent budget hotel was originally owned by a Frenchman from Toulouse (hence the name). It has a secure car park, free wi-fi and a variety of rooms, plainly decorated but always spick and span. Some have ceiling fans too. **From 300dh**

IBIS MARRAKECH CENTRE GARE MAP p.65, POCKET MAP A4. Av Hassan II/Pl de la Gare, Guéliz ☎ 0524 435929, ⓦ ibishotel. com. This tasteful chain hotel located right by the train station is not the most exciting accommodation in town, but it's good value. It offers efficient service, a swimming pool, a restaurant and a bar in the lobby, and good buffet breakfasts are available. **812dh**

LES DEUX TOURS MAP p.65, POCKET MAP J1. Douar Abiad, Circuit de la Palmeraie, 4km from town ☎ 0524 329525, ⓦ les-deux-tours.com. The *deux tours* (two towers) of the name flank the gateway to this cluster of luxury *villas d'hôte* designed by locally renowned architect Charles Boccara. Located in an open patch of the Palmery, and not signposted (take a turn-off to the east about halfway along the Route de la Palmeraie, signposted "Villa des Trois Golfs", then continue for about 600m, ignoring any further signs to the *Trois Golfs*), this is a beautiful, tranquil spot, with four rooms to each villa, all built in traditional Moroccan brick and decorated in restful earth colours, and each villa with its own little garden. There's a hammam, swimming pool, restaurant and bar, as well as extensive shared gardens in which to wander or relax. **From €229 (2455dh)**

THE RED HOUSE MAP p.65, POCKET MAP E6. Bd el Yarmouk, opposite the city wall, Hivernage ☎ 0524 437040, ⓦ theredhousemarrakech.com. This beautiful nineteenth-century mansion (also called *Dar el Ahmar*) is awash with fine stucco and zellij work downstairs, where the restaurant offers gourmet Moroccan cuisine (see p.76). Accommodation consists of eight luxurious suites – extremely chic and palatial – though imperial European rather than classic Moroccan in style. **From 2000dh**

SOFITEL MARRAKECH MAP p.65, POCKET MAP D6. Rue Harroun Errachid, Hivernage ☎ 0524 425600, Ⓦ sofitel.com. This chain hotel is not up to Western five-star standards, but it isn't too bad as package hotels go. It's done out in royal red, with two restaurants, two bars, three pools and a fitness centre with a sauna, jacuzzi and hammam. **3372dh**

YOUTH HOSTEL (AUBERGE DE JEUNESSE) MAP p.65, POCKET MAP A5. Rue el Jahed, Hivernage ☎ 0524 447713, Ⓦ hihostels. com. Friendly, quiet and sparkling clean youth hostel, with a small garden. It's also a useful first-night standby if you arrive late by train, as it's just five minutes' walk from the station. You don't need an HI card to stay here, but cardholders get priority. Breakfast not included. **Dorms 70dh**

Atlas Mountains: Imlil

HOTEL SOLEIL ☎ 0524 485622, Ⓦ hotelsoleilimlil.com. The rooms are bright but cosy and mostly en suite at this cheery little place with friendly staff and great views from the terrace. Excluding breakfast. **From 200dh**

IMLIL REFUGE ☎ 0524 484881, Ⓦ imlilrefuge.com/ImlilRefuge/. Run by "mountaineering buffs", as they call themselves, this place has small but cosy rooms. Mud and straw walls (like the inside of a traditional kasbah) give it a pleasantly rustic feel, and all the rooms have a scenic view. Excluding breakfast. **From 200dh**

KASBAH DU TOUBKAL ☎ 0524 485611, UK ☎ +44 1883 744392, Ⓦ kasbahdutoubkal.com. The former kasbah of a local *caid* (chief) lovingly restored by British tour company Discover Ltd using local craftsmen, this is Imlil's top offering and indeed its top sight. It starred as the Dalai Lama's palace in Martin Scorsese's film *Kundun*, but you don't need to be the leader of Tibet to enjoy the beautiful guest rooms or the

excellent meals, nor to take advantage of the excursions it offers, on foot or by mule. Even if you don't stay here, it's worth at least popping in for tea on the terrace. Slightly cheaper accommodation from the same firm is available at the nearby *Dar Imlil*. Rates include breakfast, use of the in-house hammam, and a donation towards local community projects. **From €170 (1775dh)**

RIAD ATLAS TOUBKAL ☎ 0662 058251, Ⓦ riadatlastoubkal.com. Great value riad-style accommodation directly above the village (just over the river, beyond the *Dar Imlil*). There are a range of rooms, all en suite, some with tubs, some with balconies, plus a big, sunny terrace on the roof. **From 300dh**

Atlas Mountains: Setti Fatma

AU BORD DE L'EAU 500m below the taxi stand ☎ 0661 229755, Ⓦ obordelo. com. You'll need to reserve well ahead to bag a room here at Setti Fatma's loveliest hostelry, beneath the road and next to the river, with a small backpackers' room and three larger rooms. The decor in the rooms is well chosen, the tables in the garden are made of old millstones, and the food is absolutely out of this world – home cooking with locally sourced ingredients, often grown on the premises. Excluding breakfast. **Backpacker room 250dh, others 350–450dh**

HOTEL NAJMA 300m below the taxi stand ☎ 0524 485757, Ⓔ najmahotel1 @gmail.com. This hotel functions as a more upmarket annexe for the *Setti Fatma* across the street (the owners are cousins). Rooms are all very simple, though fresh and new, and come in a variety of sizes; all have bathrooms, though not all have outside windows. There are also suites, and a couple of self-catering apartments on the roof (200dh for up to six people). Rate excludes breakfast. **150dh**

HOTEL-RESTAURANT ASGAOUR 200m below the taxi stand ☎ 0524 485294, Ⓦ asgaour.skyblog.com. This bright and friendly little hotel with rooms above its restaurant proudly displays its French guidebook recommendations out front. The rooms are small and plain but clean and carpeted, some en suite, and there's a sunny upper-floor terrace. Heaters are available in winter for 30dh extra. **From 150dh**

HOTEL SETTI FATMA 300m below the taxi stand ☎ 0670 106574. Formerly known as the *Hotel du Gare* because of its location by the former site of the taxi station, this is one of the oldest hotels in town. Rooms are plain, with shared bathroom facilities, but clean and comfortable; some are older and more basic, others are newer and brighter with a view over the river. There's a restaurant serving food indoors or in the garden. Breakfast excluded. **From 70dh**

Atlas Mountains: Oukaïmeden

AUBERGE DE L'ANGOUR (CHEZ JUJU) ☎ 0524 319005, Ⓦ hotelchezjuju. com. There's an old-fashioned, almost country-inn feel about this place on the main road in the centre of the village. It's nice and homely with a decent bar and restaurant; some rooms are fully en suite, but most have just an en-suite shower and a toilet on the landing. Rates exclude breakfast. **900dh**

CAF REFUGE ☎ 0524 319036. Priority is given to Club Alpin Français members at this hostel, which has the only budget accommodation in the village. You stay in a dorm and there are sheets and blankets, but you're advised to bring a sleeping bag nonetheless. Meals are also available. **Dorms 170dh (CAF members 80dh)**

Essaouira

DAR ADUL MAP p.86, POCKET MAP E10. 63 Rue Touahen ☎ 0524 473910, Ⓦ www.daradul.ma. Lashings of whitewash (with maritime blue woodwork) give this French-run riad a bright, airy feel, and help to keep it cool in summer. It has a selection of different-sized rooms – some split-level – and the biggest has a fireplace to keep it warm in winter. **From €59 (636dh)**

DAR AL BAHAR MAP p.86, POCKET MAP E10. 1 Rue Touahen ☎ 0524 476831, Ⓦ daralbahar.com. Views of the wild ocean crashing against the rocks below, especially from the terrace, plus cool whitewashed rooms, hung with paintings by some of the best local artists, make this riad an excellent choice, though it's a bit tucked away. **From 440dh**

DAR NESS MAP p.86, POCKET MAP E11. 1 Rue Khalid Ben el Oualid, just off Place Prince Moulay el Hassan ☎ 0524 476804, Ⓦ darness-essaouira.com. This is a nineteenth-century house turned into an attractive riad by its French owner, with cool, clean and well-kept rooms, brick floors and jolly little tiled bathrooms. The place is well run, but it does sometimes lack the personal touch that many people expect from a riad. **From 600dh**

HOTEL BEAU RIVAGE MAP p.86, POCKET MAP E11. 14 Pl Prince Moulay el Hassan ☎ 0524 475925. A budget hotel that tried to go upmarket but has slid back down again. It has an enviable position right on the main square – which also means that rooms at the front can be a bit noisy at times. There's a variety of charming en-suite rooms, all bright and breezy, the best of them with balconies, but it's not as well-maintained as it might be. **From 200dh**

HOTEL CAP SIM MAP p.86, POCKET MAP E11. 11 Rue Ibn Rochd ☎ 0524 785834, ⓦ hotelcapsim.com. The rooms are a little small at this popular budget hotel, but they're all clean and bright, some are en suite, and the water is partly solar-heated. The staff are extremely helpful, and there's a fourth-floor sun terrace for catching the rays with a view over the rooftops. From 220dh

HOTEL RIAD AL MEDINA MAP p.86, POCKET MAP E11. 9 Rue Attarine ☎ 0524 475907, ⓦ riadalmadina.com. This former palatial mansion, built in 1871, had fallen on hard times by the 1960s and become a budget hotel for hippies. Guests supposedly included Jimi Hendrix (in room 13 according to some stories, room 28 say others), as well as Frank Zappa, the Jefferson Airplane and Cat Stevens. Now refurbished, it has bags of character and helpful staff but it's still rather rustic in some respects (the plumbing can be temperamental for example) and it's relatively expensive for what you get. From 814dh

HOTEL SOUIRI MAP p.86, POCKET MAP E11. 37 Rue Attarine ☎ 0524 475339, ⓦ hotelsouiri.com. Deservedly popular and very central, this budget (but not *too* budget) hotel offers a range of rooms, the cheaper ones having shared bathroom facilities. The decor in the rooms is a little bit busy (paint-sponged walls to imitate wallpaper), but homely and cosy. Those at the front are considered the best, though those at the back are quieter. From 230dh

LE MÉDINA ESSAOUIRA HOTEL MAP p.86, POCKET MAP G13. Bd Mohammed V ☎ 0525 072526, ⓦ sofitel.com. This is the most expensive hotel in town by a very long chalk, and it's the place to come if you favour deluxe comforts and amenities over traditional charm and character. Its facilities include a pool, two bars, two restaurants, serving fish and local cuisine, and a thalassotherapy centre (just in case a good, old-fashioned swim in the sea isn't thalassotherapeutic enough). Rooms have a light and airy feel, with a stylish cookies-and-cream colour scheme. From 1600dh

RIAD BAB ESSAOUIRA MAP p.86, POCKET MAP E10. 35 bis, Bd Moulay Abderrahmane Eddakhil ☎ 0524 785508, ⓦ riad-bab-essaouira.com. This small, well-managed and very stylish riad offers suites only, decorated throughout in cool white with brown and black trimmings and a subtle Afro-Gnaoua theme. Each suite occupies one floor, and includes a sitting room and a bathroom with individual water heater. The rooftop suite has its own small terrace. There's a communal salon and a self-catering kitchen. From €50 (545dh)

RIAD LE GRAND LARGE MAP p.86, POCKET MAP F10. 2 Rue Oum Rabia ☎ 0524 476886, ⓔ contact@riadlegrandlarge.com. Despite its name, this is a small, cosy place with ten smallish rooms. Staff are lovely, the restaurant is classy, there's a roof-terrace café and it's good value, with reductions off-season. The best room is the one on the roof terrace. 450dh

VILLA MAROC MAP p.86, POCKET MAP E11. 10 Rue Abdallah Ben Yassin, just inside the Medina wall near the clocktower ☎ 0524 473147, ⓦ villa-maroc.com. Established long before riads became trendy, this is an upmarket one made up of two old houses converted into a score of rooms and suites. It's decorated with the finest Moroccan materials and has its own hammam. Though it's accessible only on foot, there are porters on hand to carry your luggage from the car park in Place Orson Welles. Most of the year you will need to book several months ahead to stay here. From €80 (870dh)

ESSENTIALS

Souk in the Medina

Arrival

Most visitors arrive in Marrakesh by air, but the night train from Tangier (the "Marrakesh Express") is also a good option, and you can get to Marrakesh by train, bus or shared *grand taxi* from other parts of Morocco too.

By air

Menara airport (☏ 0524 447410) is 4km southwest of town. The arrivals hall has ATMs, and bank kiosks to change money. You won't be stranded even if neither are operating: taxis will accept euros (and sometimes dollars or sterling) at more or less the equivalent dirham rate, or you can have them call by an ATM en route to your destination.

    Petits taxis run from in front of the airport terminal. There is an (artificially high) fixed rate of 70dh (100dh at night) from the airport to the Jemaa el Fna or central Guéliz, though taxi drivers may still try to overcharge you – you should not pay above this (it's already more than double what you'd pay on the meter). Shared **grands taxis**, which also wait in front of the airport building, should charge 105dh (150dh at night) for up to six passengers for the trip to the Jemaa el Fna, Guéliz and Hivernage. **Bus** #19 (30dh one-way; 50dh return, valid for two weeks) leaves half-hourly (6.30am–9.30pm) from the stop in front of the airport terminal for Place Foucault (by the Koutoubia) and Avenue Mohammed V (Guéliz).

By train

The **train station** (☏ 0524 449777) is a ten- to fifteen-minute walk from the centre of Guéliz, or a longer walk or bus ride from the Medina; the taxi fare should be around 15dh to the Medina, less to hotels in Guéliz. Buses #8, #10,

#14 and #66 run to Place Foucault, alongside the Jemaa el Fna, across Avenue Hassan II at the corner of Rue Ezzoubair.

By bus or shared taxi

The **gare routière** (for long-distance bus services other than the national bus firm CTM, or the train company's Supratours buses) is just outside the walls of the Medina by Bab Doukkala. Most long-distance collective **grands taxis** arriving in Marrakesh terminate immediately behind this bus station, though they may drop you off in front of it on Place el Mourabitine. You can walk into the centre of Guéliz from the *gare routière* in around ten minutes by following Avenue des Nations Unies (to the right as you exit the bus station, then straight on bearing right). To the Jemaa el Fna it's around 25 minutes: follow the Medina walls (to your left as you exit the bus station) down to Avenue Mohammed V, then turn left. A *petit taxi* is about 10dh to the Jemaa el Fna, less to Guéliz. Alternatively, catch bus #6 or #16 from outside the bus station, which runs through the heart of Guéliz, or buses #8, #10, #12, #14, #15, #16, #17 or #66, which stop opposite Bab Doukkala itself (though the bus stop displays only the numbers #11 and #11B) and head south to Place Foucault.

    Supratours services from Essaouira, Agadir and the Western Sahara arrive on Avenue Hassan II next to the train station (accessed via platform 1). **CTM** services stop at their office on Rue Abou Bakr Seddik, two blocks south of Supratours. Shared *grands taxis* from the **High Atlas villages** of Asni, Imlil and Setti Fatma arrive at Rue Oqba Ben Nafaa, off Avenue Houman el Fetouaki south of the Koutoubia (see map p.28). Shared taxis from Lagarb (where you may have to change vehicles on the way down from Setti Fatma if there are no direct ones) and some from Setti Fatma, arrive nearby, on Rue Ibn Rachid. Coming from the ski resort of Oukaïmeden, unless you charter a taxi, you'll probably have to change vehicles at Lagarb.

Note that on long-distance bus journeys you're expected to tip the **porters** who load your baggage onto buses (5dh – except on CTM, which charges by weight).

Getting around

Despite its size and the maze of its souks, Marrakesh is not too hard to navigate. Inside the Medina, walking will generally be your best option, partly because most streets are too narrow to navigate in a vehicle, and partly because negotiating the Medina on foot – including getting lost a few times – is all part of the Marrakesh experience. It's true that you could get from, for example, the Jemaa el Fna to the Saadian Tombs in a taxi, but you are only likely to if you are not sufficiently fit or able-bodied to manage the journey on foot.

Between the Medina and the Ville Nouvelle, though the distance is certainly not beyond the reach of shanks's pony, you will probably find it more comfortable to take a cab, or even a bus.

Petits taxis

Other than inside the Medina, the easiest way to get around town is in one of the city's beige **petits taxis**. These take up to three passengers and are equipped with a meter; if the driver doesn't use it, it's because he intends to overcharge you. Most trips around town (petits taxis are not allowed beyond the city limits) should cost around 10–20dh during the day, or 15–30dh at night, when there is a surcharge on the meter

price. Special fares apply to and from the airport (see opposite). If you're a lone passenger, it's standard practice for the driver to pick up one or two additional passengers en route, each of whom will pay the full fare for their journey, as will you. There are petit taxi ranks at most major intersections in Guéliz, and in the Medina at the junction of Avenue Houman el Fetouaki and Rue Oqba Ben Nafaa, and at the Place des Ferblantiers end of Avenue Houman el Fetouaki. **Tuk-tuks** (like Indian auto-rickshaws) can be picked up at the Jemaa el Fna, but they're less comfortable and more expensive than petits taxis.

Bike rental

An alternative to a petit taxi for exploring the more scattered sights, such as the Agdal and Menara gardens or the Palmery, is a **bicycle**, **moped** or **scooter**. Marrakesh has a bicycle rental scheme with twelve places around town where you can pick up and deposit bicycles (50dh/day), but you'll need to register first, at ⓦ medinabike.ma. Mopeds and scooters can be rented from firms such as Loc2Roues on the upper floor of Galerie Élite, 212 Av Mohammed V (ⓣ 0524 430294, ⓦ loc2roues.com) at around 250–300dh a day for a moped or scooter. Marrakech City Bike Tour, in the same yard as the Hotel Toulousain and Café du Livre (ⓣ 0667 797035, ⓦ marrakech-city-bike-tour.com) which does 2hr 30min bicycle tours daily at 10am for 250dh (they provide the bikes).

Getting around town by bike is easy, but be aware that Moroccan drivers are not the world's best. In particular, do not expect them to observe lane discipline, nor to indicate when turning or changing lanes so always exercise particular caution when cycling in town.

Grands taxis

Grands taxis – typically large Mercedes – usually run as shared taxis, taking six passengers (though they're only designed for four) for a fixed price. You'll probably only want to use a *grand taxi* if you're heading to the **Atlas mountains** or to **Essaouira**, but if there are four, five or six of you (too many for a *petit taxi*), you might charter a *grand taxi* for use in town. You'll need to agree the price beforehand.

Shared *grands taxis (taxi collectif)* for most intercity destinations (including Essaouira) leave from just outside the city walls behind the bus station. When you arrive, ask which vehicle is going to your destination and, unless you want to charter the whole taxi, make clear that you just want individual seats (*une place* for one person, *deux places* for two and so on).

Shared *grands taxis* are fast for journeys out of town, but they are cramped and drivers are prone to speeding and dangerous overtaking. They have more than their fair share of crashes in a country where the road accident rate is already high. A lot of accidents involve shared *grand taxi* drivers falling asleep at the wheel at night, so you may wish to avoid taking one after dark.

Calèches

Calèches – horse-drawn cabs – line up near the Koutoubia, the El Badi Palace, Place de la Liberté and some of the fancier hotels. They take up to five people and are not much more expensive than *petits taxis* – though be sure to fix the price in advance, particularly if you want a tour of the town. Expect to pay around 150dh/hr or 200–300dh for a tour round the Medina walls, but you'll need to bargain hard.

Buses

City buses (ⓦ alsa.ma) are cheap and efficient, with most fares in town costing 4dh. The routes you are most

Sightseeing bus tour

If you don't have much time and you want to scoot around Marrakesh's major sights in a day or two, the hop-on hop-off **Marrakech Bus Touristique** could be for you (ⓦ alsa.ma/fr/bus-touristique). Using open-top double-deckers, with a commentary in several languages including English, the tour follows two circular routes: the first tours the **Medina and Guéliz**, calling at Place Foucault (for the Jemaa and Koutoubia), Place des Ferblantiers (for the Bahia and El Badi Palaces, plus the Mellah), Bab Agnaou (for the Saadian Tombs) and the Menara gardens; the second tours the **Palmery**, following the Circuit de la Palmeraie, and also calls at the Majorelle Garden.

The Medina/Guéliz bus departs from Place Abdelmoumen Ben Ali in Guéliz and Place Foucault in the Medina every twenty to thirty minutes from 9am till 7pm; the Palmery bus leaves from Place Abdelmoumen Ben Ali hourly 1–5pm. You can get on and off where you like, and **tickets** (145dh for one day, 190dh for two, 30dh and 50dh respectively for disabled passengers) can be bought on board, or from ticket sellers at Place Abdelmoumen Ben Ali or Place Foucault. They are valid for 24 or 48 hours, so even if you start your tour after lunch, you can finish it the following morning.

Guides

A local guide can help you find things in the Medina, and a good guide can provide some interesting commentary, but you certainly don't need one. Armed with this book and the accompanying map, you can easily find your way around Marrakesh and check out all the sights on your own. Should you want one however, the ONMT (see p.120) can put you in touch. They typically charge around 200–300dh per day. Although it's illegal to work as an unofficial guide, unlicensed guides can be found in the Jemaa el Fna, and will suddenly appear almost anywhere in the Medina if you're seen looking perplexed.

When hiring a guide, be precise about exactly what you want to see and, with an unlicensed guide, agree a fee very clearly at the outset. Whether official or not, most guides will want to steer you into shops which pay them **commission** on anything you buy (added to your shopping bill, of course). Be wary as this commission is not small – official guides quite commonly demand as much as fifty percent. You should therefore make it very clear from the start if you do not want to visit any shops or carpet "museums". Don't be surprised if your guide subsequently loses interest or tries to raise the fee.

likely to want to use are #1 and #16, which run along Avenue Mohammed V between Guéliz and the Koutoubia. Other handy routes include #6 from Place Foucault (by the Koutoubia) via Bab Ighli to the Agdal Gardens, #11 from Place Youssef Tachfine to the Menara gardens and #19 from Place Foucault and Guéliz to the airport. You pay fares to the driver on board.

Directory A–Z

Cinemas

In Guéliz, the **Colisée**, opposite *La Taverne* on Bd Mohammed Zerktouni (☎ 0524 448893), is one of the best in town. In the Medina, there's the **Cinéma Mabrouka** on Rue Bab Agnaou (☎ 0524 443303). **Cinéma Eden** on Rue Riad Zitoun el Jedid was a more downmarket picture house but is now being upgraded as part of a local development.

Consulates

The **UK Honorary Consulate** is at Borj Menara 2, Immeuble B, 5th Floor, at the northern end of Av Abdelkrim el Khattabi (☎ 0537 633333). Nationalities represented in Rabat include the **US** (☎ 0537 637200), **Canada** (☎ 0537 544949; also representing **Australians**) and **South Africa** (☎ 0537 689159). **Ireland** has a Casablanca consulate (☎ 0522 272721).

Cookery courses

The **Maison Arabe** (see p.50 & p.100) offers workshops in Moroccan cooking for groups of up to eight people, at 600dh per person. **Amal Restaurant Solidaire** (see p.72) is cheaper, or there's the **Rhode School of Cuisine** (UK ☎ +44 20 7193 1221, US ☎ 1 888 254 1070, ⌨ rhodeschoolofcuisine. co.uk), who offer week-long courses from €2145 per person, including villa accommodation in the Palmery and meals on site.

Emergency numbers

Police ☎ 19
Tourist police ☎ 0524 384601
Fire or ambulance ☎ 15
SOS Médecins ☎ 0524 404040

Crime

Dial ☎ 19 for the **police**. The **tourist police** (*brigade touristique*; ☎ 0524 384601) are based on the west side of the Jemaa el Fna.

The crime rate in Marrakesh is very low and you are extremely unlikely to be mugged. **Pickpocketing** is more common, especially on crowded buses and in the crowds around performers in the Jemaa el Fna, and you should always keep an eye on your baggage in the train and bus stations. Various little **scams** are practised on tourists, which you may consider harmless; for example, people who ask what you are looking for in the Medina (usually when you are not obviously looking for anything) do so in order to insist on leading you to whatever place you name so that they can then demand payment for it.

Some **women travellers** experience a lot of **sexual harassment** in Marrakesh, while others have little or no trouble. The obvious strategies for getting rid of unwanted attention are the same as you would use at home: appear confident and assured, and you'll avoid a lot of trouble. Avoid physical contact with Moroccan men, even in a manner that would not be considered sexual at home, since it could easily be misunderstood. On the other hand, if a Moroccan man touches you he has definitely crossed the line, and you should not be afraid to **make a scene**. Shouting *shooma!* ("shame on you!") is likely to result in bystanders intervening on your behalf.

Customs allowances

One litre of wine, one of spirits, and 200 cigarettes or 200g of tobacco for each adult.

Electricity

The supply is 220v 50Hz. Sockets have two round pins as in Europe. You should be able to find adaptors in Morocco that will take North American plugs (but North American appliances may need a transformer, unless multi-voltage). Adaptors for British and Australasian plugs will need to be brought from home.

Golf

Marrakesh has half a dozen eighteen-hole golf courses, including: the **Marrakesh Royal Golf Club** (☎ 0524 409828, ⊛ royalgolfmarrakech. com), 5km southeast of town on the old Ouarzazate road, which is Morocco's oldest course, opened in 1923 and once played on by the likes of Churchill, Lloyd George and Eisenhower; the **Palmeraie Golf Club** (☎ 0524 368766, ⊛ palmgolfclub marrakech.com), built, as the name suggests, in the Palmery, off the Route de Casablanca, northeast of town; and the **Assoufid Golf Club**, 10km southwest of town on Route Guemassa, beyond the airport (☎ 0525 060770, ⊛ assoufid.com). All courses are open to non-members, with green fees at 400–850dh per day.

Health

Dr Abdelmajid Ben Tbib, 171 Av Mohammed V, Guéliz (☎ 0524 431030), and Dr Frédéric Reitzer, Immeuble Berdaï (entrance C, 2nd floor, apt 10), at the corner of Av Mohammed V and Av Moulay el Hassan, Guéliz (☎ 0524 439562), are recommended **doctors**. There's also an **emergency call-out service**, SOS Médecins (☎ 0524 404040), which charges 500dh per consultation; the emergency ambulance number is ☎15. **Private clinics** accustomed to settling bills with insurance companies include Polyclinique du Sud, at the corner of Rue de Yougoslavie and Rue Ibn Aïcha, Guéliz (☎0524 447999), and Clinique Yasmine, 12 Rue Ibn Toumert (☎0524 439694).

Dr Abdel-Jaouad Bennani, on the first floor of 112 Av Mohammed V (☎0524 449136), opposite the ONMT office in Guéliz, is a recommended **dentist** and speaks some English.

There are several **pharmacies** along Av Mohammed V; the Pharmacie de la Liberté, just off Pl de la Liberté, is a good one. In the Medina, try Pharmacie de la Place and Pharmacie du Progrés on Rue Bab Agnaou just off the Jemaa el Fna. There's an **all-night pharmacy** (*depot de nuit*) by the Tourist Police on the Jemaa el Fna and another on Rue Khalid Ben Oualid near the fire station in Guéliz. Late-opening and weekend outlets (*pharmacies de garde*) are listed in pharmacy windows.

Internet

The best place to get online is at the **Moulay Abdeslam Cyber-Park**, on Av Mohammed V opposite the Ensemble Artisanal (daily 10am–7pm, Ramadan 10am–4.30pm), which has fast connections and low rates (5dh/hr). Also, almost the entire park is a free wi-fi zone, with the best connectivity near the fountain in the middle.

Internet cafés (*cybers*, pronounced "sea bear") near the **Jemaa el Fna** include Cybercom, upstairs at 34 Rue Bani Marine (daily 8am–midnight; 7dh/hr), Katb Amoumi on Rue Kennaria (9.30am–midnight; 10dh/hr). In **Guéliz**, internet cafés are surprisingly thin on the ground; try Cyber 4 Megas, at the end of the arcade at 115 Rue de Yougoslavie (daily 9am–10pm; 5dh/hr), or Cyber Ahmed, in Passage Ghandoui at 10 Bd Mohammed Zerktouni by La Taverne restaurant (daily 10am–10pm; 6dh/hr).

Haggling

Like it or not, for most crafts you buy, you're expected to **haggle**. Contrary to popular belief, there's no magic percentage of the opening price to aim for, but you should always know before you begin how much you want to pay. If the shopkeeper's opening price is higher, respond by offering somewhat less than what you had in mind, and let them argue you up, but not above the price you've decided. If the seller will come down to that, then you have a deal; if not, no damage is done (and you can always think about it and come back the next day). Bear in mind too that, as at an auction, if you state a price and the seller agrees, you are morally obliged to pay, so never let a figure pass your lips that you are not prepared to pay, and don't start haggling for something if you don't really want it.

Haggling is a social activity, and should always be good-natured, never acrimonious, even if you know that the seller is trying to overcharge you outrageously. Theatrics are all part of the game, and buyers' tactics can include pointing to flaws, talking of lower quotes received elsewhere, feigning indifference, or having a friend urge you to leave. Avoid being tricked into raising your bid twice in a row or admitting your estimate of the object's worth (just reply that you've made your offer). If you want to check out the going rates before you shop, visit the Ensemble Artisanal (see p.46) or Entreprise Bouchaib (see p.59), where prices are fixed if a little high.

Laundry

Most hotels offer a laundry service. In the smaller, budget hotels, this may simply be a question of coming to a private arrangement with the cleaners (who'll be laundering the bedding anyway). Failing that, there are laundries and dry cleaners dotted around town. Try Pressing Oasis, 44 Rue Tarik Ibn Zaid, Guéliz (two doors from *Hôtel Toulousain*).

LGBT+ travellers

Gay sex between men is illegal in Morocco, and attitudes to it are different from those in the West. A Moroccan who takes the dominant role in gay intercourse may well not consider himself to be indulging in a homosexual act, but the idea of being a passive partner, on the other hand, is virtually taboo. A certain amount of cruising goes on in the crowds of the Jemaa el Fna in the evening. A number of riads are run by gay male couples, but very few by lesbian couples, and there is no perceptible lesbian scene in Marrakesh as yet. The 2014 arrest of a British man and his Moroccan alleged gay lover still underlines the need for discretion, as does the 2016 arrest of two teenage girls for kissing after the mother of one of them reported it to the police.

Money

Morocco's unit of currency is the **dirham** (dh), which at the time of writing was selling at approximately 12.20dh for £1, 9.30dh for US$1, 11.20dh for €1. As with all currencies there are fluctuations, but the dirham has held its own against Western currencies over the last few years. The dirham is divided into 100 **centimes** or francs, and you may find prices written or expressed in centimes rather than dirhams. Confusingly, prices are sometimes quoted in **rials**, one rial being five centimes. Coins of 10, 20 and 50 centimes, and 1, 5 and 10 dirhams are in circulation, along with notes of 20, 25, 50, 100 and 200 dirhams. It is illegal to import or export more than 2000dh, and dirhams are not easily obtainable abroad anyway.

US and Canadian dollars and pounds sterling (Bank of England – not Scottish or Northern Irish notes) are easily exchangeable at Marrakesh **banks**, but **euros** are by far the best hard currency to carry, since they are not only easy to change, but are accepted as cash very widely, at the rate of €1 for 11dh.

The best way to carry your money is in the form of **plastic**, which – if it belongs to the Visa, MasterCard, Cirrus and Plus networks – can be used to withdraw cash from **ATMs** across town. Make sure before you leave home that your cards and PINs will work overseas. You can also settle bills in upmarket hotels, restaurants and tourist shops using MasterCard, Visa or American Express cards. There is a daily limit on ATM withdrawals, usually 4000dh. Using plastic in ATMs gives you better exchange rates than changing cash in banks, but your card issuer may add a transaction fee of as much as 5.5 percent.

The main area for **banks** in the Medina is off the south side of the Jemaa el Fna on Rue Moulay Ismail and Rue Bab Agnaou. In Guéliz, aim for Av Mohammed V between Pl Abdelmoumen Ben Ali and the market. Most major branches have ATMs that will accept foreign cards. **Banking hours** are typically Mon–Fri 8.15am–3.45pm (9.30am–2pm during Ramadan). Most BMCE branches are open Mon–Fri 9.15am–5.45pm (Ramadan 9.15am–2.30pm), and their branch in the Medina (Rue Moulay Ismail on Pl Foucauld) has a bureau de change open daily 10am–noon & 3.30–7pm. **Post offices** will also change cash, and there are an increasing

number of **private forex bureaux.**
There are also plenty of private foreign
exchange bureaux around town,
typically open daily 10am–10pm,
including one off the Jemaa el Fna on
Rue Riad Zitoun el Kedim at Derb Sidi
Bouloukat, and one at the *Hotel Farouk*
in Guéliz (see p.105). Out of hours,
Hotel Ali (see p.96) and *Hotel Central
Palace* (see p.97) will change money.
The *Hotel Ali* often has the best rates
in town in any case.

Opening hours

Shops in the Medina tend to open every
day from 9am to 6pm, with some closed
for lunch (around 1–3pm), especially
on a Friday. In the Ville Nouvelle, shops
are more likely to close for lunch, but
tend to stay open later, until 7 or 8pm,
and to close on Sundays. **Offices** are
usually open Monday to Thursday
8.30am to noon and 2.30 to 6.30pm; on
Friday their hours are typically 8.30 to
11.30am and 3 to 6.30pm. **Restaurants**
generally open between noon and 3pm,
and again from 7 to 11pm; only the
cheaper places stay open through the
afternoon.

All these opening hours change
completely during the holy month of
Ramadan (see p.122), when Muslims
fast from daybreak to nightfall. At this
time, shops, offices and banks close
early (3–4pm) to allow staff to go
home to break the fast. Restaurants
may close completely during Ramadan,
or open after dusk only, though a
couple of places on the Jemaa el
Fna will be open through the day to
serve tourists.

Phones

You may well be able to use your
mobile phone in Marrakesh, though
US phones need to be GSM to work
abroad. Note that once in Marrakesh
you'll pay to receive calls as well as to
make them. Prepaid cards from abroad
cannot be charged up or replaced
locally, but you can get a Moroccan
number with a **local SIM** card (20dh
plus ID), available, along with top-ups,
from *téléboutiques* and offices of
Maroc Telecom and Méditel.

Another way to make a call is to use
a **téléboutique**, where you usually use
coins; *téléboutiques* are dotted around
town, including one at 65 Rue Bab
Agnaou, opposite *Hotel Central Palace*.
Calling direct from your hotel room is
obviously more convenient, but will
cost a lot more.

To **call abroad from Morocco**,
dial ☏ 0044 for the UK, ☏ 00353 for
Ireland, ☏ 0061 for Australia and
☏ 0064 for New Zealand, followed by
the area code (minus the initial zero)
and the number. To call North America,
dial ☏ 001, then the three-digit area
code, then the number. When **calling
Marrakesh from abroad**, dial the
international access code, then
country code for Morocco, ☏ 212,
followed by the number – omitting the
initial zero.

If you're **calling within Morocco**,
note that Moroccan area codes have
been scrapped, and that all Moroccan
phones, including mobiles, have a
ten-digit number, all digits of which
must be dialled. Marrakesh landline
numbers begin 0524.

Post

The main **post office** (*la poste* in French, *el boosta* or *el barid* in Arabic) is on Pl 16 Novembre, midway down Av Mohammed V in Guéliz (Mon–Fri 8am–4pm, Sat 8.30am–noon for poste restante and full services). Stamps are also sold and money changed (Mon–Fri 8am–6pm, Sat 8.30am–noon). The Medina has a branch post office on the Jemaa el Fna (Mon–Fri 8am–6pm, Sat 10am–6pm), one opposite the Bahia Palace on Rue Riad Zitoun el Jedid (Mon–Fri 8am–4.15pm), and another in the train station (Mon–Fri 8am–4.15pm).

Smoking

Cigarettes are cheap in Morocco and most men smoke. There are few restrictions on smoking, and those who cannot tolerate others smoking around them will be hard put to find non-smoking areas. On the other hand it is not considered respectable for women to smoke in public, and doing so will look tarty to Moroccans. **Cannabis** is cheap and widely used (dealers offer it to tourists in the back streets south of the Jemaa el Fna), but it is illegal, and buying it lays you open to set-ups and possible arrest.

Swimming pools

Many hotels allow non-residents to use their pools including the **Grand Hotel Tazi** south of the Jemaa el Fna (100dh) and **Hotel Akabar** (Av Echouhada, Hivernage, near Bab Nkob; ☎0524 437799; 60dh). Handy if you're with kids who hate sightseeing is **Oasiria**, at km4, Route du Barrage, on the Asni/Oumnass road (daily 10am–6pm; 210dh, children under 1.5m and senior citizens 130dh ☎0524 380438, ⓦoasiria.com); it even runs free shuttle buses from town from mid-June to August. The *Palmeraie Golf Palace* hotel runs a more expensive place called **Nikki Beach** (daily 11.30am–8pm; 300dh; ☎0663 519992, ⓦnikkibeach.com) in the Palmery.

Time

Morocco is on Greenwich Mean Time (GMT/UTC), with daylight saving (GMT+1) from the last Sunday of March until the last Sunday of October, but reverting to GMT during Ramadan until the end of the Aid es Seghir. Otherwise, the time is the same in Marrakesh as in Britain and Ireland, five hours ahead of the US east coast (EST) and eight ahead of the west coast (PST). In principle, Marrakesh is two hours behind South Africa, eight hours behind Australia's west coast, ten hours behind eastern Australia, and twelve hours behind New Zealand.

Tipping

You're expected to tip waiters in cafés (1–2dh per person) and restaurants (5–10dh or so in moderate places, 10–15 percent in upmarket places). Taxi drivers do not expect a tip but always appreciate one of course.

Tourist information

The **Moroccan National Tourist Office** (Office National Marocain de Tourisme in French or ONMT for short; ⓦvisitmorocco.com) has offices in several Western cities including London (☎020 7437 0073, ✉mnto@morocco-tourism.org.uk), New York (☎1 212 221 1583 ✉info@mnto-usa.org) and Montreal (☎1 514 842 8111, ✉onmt@qc.aira.com).

The ONMT office in Marrakesh, also called the **Délégation Régional du Tourisme**, is on Pl Abdelmoumen Ben Ali in Guéliz (Mon–Fri 8.30am–4.30pm; ☎0524 436131). For online listings, see the Marrakech Travel Guide website at ⓦtravelmarrakech.co.uk.

Public holidays

Public holidays include: Aid el Kebir and Aid es Seghir, which run for two days each (see p.122); New Year's Day (Jan 1); Anniversary of the Istiqlal Party's 1944 independence manifesto (Jan 11); Labour Day (May 1); Feast of the Throne (July 30); Allegiance Day (Aug 14); King and People's Revolution Day (Aug 20); King's Birthday and Youth Day (Aug 21); Anniversary of the Green March to occupy the Western Sahara (Nov 6); and Independence Day (Nov 18).

Travellers with children

Moroccan streets are pretty safe and even quite small children walk to school unaccompanied or play in the street unsupervised. As a parent however, you will encounter one or two difficulties. For example, you won't find **baby changing rooms** in hotels or restaurants, and will have to be discreet if **breastfeeding**. Riads tend to have an adult atmosphere, and some even ban children, so you may want to stay at one of the chain hotels in Hivernage (see p.105), which have, apart from anything else, swimming pools. Disposable **nappies** (diapers) are available at supermarkets and some pharmacies. Remember that children are more susceptible than adults to heatstroke and dehydration, so pack a sunhat, and some high-factor **sunscreen**. Wet wipes are also very handy things to take.

Travellers with disabilities

Marrakesh is not a tremendously accessible city but Moroccans are generally more used to mixing with and helping people with disabilities than their Western counterparts, and taxis are also a lot more affordable. The Ville Nouvelle is generally easier to negotiate than the Medina, but don't expect kerb ramps at road crossings or other such concessions. There is little wheelchair access to most budget hotels or riads, and wheelchair users may be forced to stay in the chain hotels in Hivernage. Hotels that have rooms adapted for wheelchair users include the *Atlas Medina* (see p.105), and the *Grand Mogador Menara* (see p.105), as well as the *Le Médina Essaouira* in Essaouira (see p.109).

Vegetarian food

Awareness of vegetarianism is gradually increasing, especially in places used to dealing with tourists, but meat stock and animal fat are widely used in cooking, even in dishes that do not contain meat as such, but not in dishes that are specifically described as vegetarian. Increasingly, restaurants that are popular with tourists are offering vegetarian versions of couscous, tajine and even pastilla, and the *Earth Café* (see p.32) has vegetarian and vegan food. Otherwise, the cheaper restaurants serve omelettes, salads and sometimes *bisara* (pea soup), with fancier restaurants offering good salads and sometimes pizza. "I'm a vegetarian" is *ana nabaati* in Arabic, or *je suis vegetarien/vegetarienne* in French. You could add: *la akulu lehoum (wala hout)* in Arabic, or *je ne mange aucune sorte de viande (ni poisson)* in French, both meaning "I don't eat any kind of meat (or fish)".

Festivals and events

Marrakesh's most important celebrations are religious holidays, fixed according to the Islamic lunar calendar. Dates for these in the Western (Gregorian) calendar cannot be predicted exactly as they depend on monthly moon sightings, so they may vary by a day or two from the approximate dates given here.

Marrakesh Marathon

January ⓦ marathon-marrakech.com.
More than 5000 athletes from Morocco and abroad come to run this gruelling but scenic 42km race around the Medina and through the Palmery on the third or fourth Sunday of the month.

Ramadan

Late April or May
Practising Muslims fast from dawn to sunset in the holy month of Ramadan; the fast is then broken each evening with a meal that traditionally features soup, dates and eggs. Ramadan starts around 16 May 2018, 6 May 2019, 24 April 2020 and 13 April 2021.

Essaouira Gnaoua Festival

May or June ⓦ festival-gnaoua.net.
This annual music festival in Essaouira is held to celebrate the music of the Gnaoua Sufi brotherhood, which originated among slaves brought to Morocco from Senegal and Mali. See p.88.

Aid es Seghir

May or June
Also called Aid el Fitr, this two-day feast and public holiday celebrates the end of Ramadan. It will be held on approximately 15 June 2018, 5 June 2019, 24 May 2020 and 13 May 2021.

Festival National des Arts Populaires

June or July ⓦ facebook.com/Festival-National-des-Arts-Populaires-184828808346920.
Marrakesh's biggest annual cultural event features performances by musicians and dancers from Morocco and beyond in the El Badi Palace and other venues, plus displays of horsemanship each evening at Bab Jedid.

Setti Fatma Moussem

August
A four-day annual shindig held in commemoration of a local saint in the Ourika Valley's main village, with a large market, fair, sideshows and Berber and Sufi dancing. See p.82.

Aid el Kebir

July or August
To celebrate the prophet Abraham's willingness to sacrifice his son to God, Muslim families (if they can afford it) buy and slaughter a sheep, which they eat over the next two days – you will see a lot of people leading sheep around town in the run-up to the festival. Probable dates (depending on moon sightings) are: 22 August 2018, 12 August 2019, 31 July 2020 and 20 July 2021.

Marrakesh Film Festival

Late November or early December
ⓦ festivalmarrakech.info.
Marrakesh's big cinematic event is increasingly important on the international circuit, with movies shown at cinemas across town, and on large screens in the El Badi Palace and the Jemaa el Fna. The films shown come from all over the world, but with an emphasis on Moroccan, African and Arab cinema.

Chronology

681 AD Oqba Ibn Nafi brings Islam to Morocco.

787 Moulay Idriss establishes an Arab kingdom in Morocco; Arabs migrate into the country and Arabic becomes the language at court.

1062–70 Marrakesh is founded by the Almoravids, a Berber religious fundamentalist movement led by Youssef Ben Tachfine, who makes the new city his capital.

1126–27 First city walls constructed.

1147 Marrakesh falls to the Almohads, another Berber religious movement, who destroy most Almoravid constructions.

1172 Almohads take control of Andalusia (Muslim Spain).

1184 Yacoub el Mansour takes the throne, heralding Marrakesh's golden age. Poets and scholars arrive at court.

1269 Marrakesh falls to the Merenid dynasty, whose capital is Fez.

1472 Wattasid dynasty (formerly viziers to the Merenids) takes power.

1492 Fall of last Islamic kingdom in Spain forces Andalusian refugees into Morocco.

1521 Marrakesh is taken by a new regime, the Saadians, who make it their capital.

1557 First burial at what is to become the Saadian Tombs.

1558 Mellah (Jewish quarter) established.

1578–1603 Under Ahmed el Mansour, Marrakesh sees a last burst of imperial splendour. El Badi Palace constructed.

1672 Alaouite sultan Moulay Ismail takes power and moves the capital to Meknes.

1792 The "mad sultan" Moulay Yazid becomes the last person to be buried in the Saadian Tombs.

1866–67 Bahia Palace built for Sultan Moulay Hassan's grand vizier Si Moussa.

1912 French "protectorate" established. Despite resistance led by local chieftain El Hiba, French forces occupy Marrakesh and begin construction of the Ville Nouvelle.

1918 T'hami el Glaoui appointed pasha of Marrakesh by the French colonialists.

1956 Morocco becomes independent under Mohammed V, who re-establishes monarchical rule.

1969 Jimi Hendrix visits Marrakesh and Essaouira.

1980s and 90s Migration from rural areas swells the city's population. Marrakesh re-establishes itself as Morocco's second biggest city after Casablanca.

2000s Huge rise in tourism, growth of riad industry, expansion of suburbs north and west of town.

2011 Bomb attack at the *Restaurant Argana* (see p.35).

2015 *Restaurant Argana* re-opens

2016 Two teenage girls arrested for kissing but released after worldwide outcry.

Language

The most important language in Marrakesh is **Moroccan Arabic**, as different from the Arabic of the Middle East as Jamaican Patwa is from British or American English. Many Marrakshis speak **Tashelhait** (also called Chleuh), the local Berber language, and most also speak French.

Pronunciation

In our Arabic transliteration below, we've used **kh** to represent the sound of ch in "loch", and **gh** to represent a gargling sound similar to a French "r". A **q** represents a "k" pronounced in the back of the throat rather than a "kw", and **j** is like the "zh" in Dr Zhivago; **r** should be trilled, as in Spanish. In Arabic words of more than one syllable, the stressed syllable is shown in bold.

Words and phrases

Even if you learn no other Arabic phrases, it's useful to know the all-purpose greeting, *assalaam aleikum* ("peace to you"); the reply is *waaleikum salaam* ("and to you peace"). When speaking of anything in the future, Moroccans usually say *insha'allah* ("God willing"), and when talking of any kind of good fortune, they say *alhamdulillah* ("praise be to God"). It is normal to respond to these expressions by repeating them. If you really want to impress people, you could try some Tashelhait: "hello" is *manzakin* (with the stress on the second syllable) and "thank you" is *tanmeert*.

Below are some basic Arabic and French vocabulary for everyday communication. You may find it handy to supplement this list with a phrasebook, such as the *Rough Guide French Phrasebook*. Both Arabic and French use genders, even for inanimate objects, and the word ending varies slightly according to the gender.

Basics

English	Arabic	French
yes	**eyeh, na**am	oui
no	la	non
I/me	**e**na	moi
you (m/f)	**en**ta/**en**tee	vous
he/him	**hoo**wa	lui
she/her	**hee**ya	elle
we/us	**neh**noo	nous
they	hoom	ils/elles
(very) good	mez**yen** (bzef)	(très) bon
big	ke**beer**	grand
small	seg**heer**	petit
old	ke**deem**	vieux
new	je**deed**	nouveaux
a little	**shwee**ya	un peu
a lot	bzef	beaucoup
open	mah**lul**	ouvert
closed	mas**dud**	fermé
hello/how's it going?	le **bes**?	ça va?
good morning	sbah l'**kheer**	bonjour
good evening	msa l'**kheer**	bon soir
good night	**lei**la sa**ee**da	bonne nuit
goodbye	bise**la**ma	au revoir
who...?	sh**koon**...?	qui...?
when...?	**im**ta...?	quand...?
why...?	a**lash**...?	pourquoi...?
how...?	ki**fesh**...?	comment...?
which/what...?	sh**noo**...?	quel...?
is there...?	kayn...?	est-ce qu'il y a...?
do you have...?	an**dak**.../kayn...?	avez-vous...?
please	**af**ak/min **fad**lak *to a man or* **af**ik /min**fad**lik *to a woman*	s'il vous plaît
thank you	**shuk**ran	merci
ok/agreed	**wa**kha	d'accord
that's enough/ that's all	**sa**fee	ça suffit
excuse me	is**mah**lee	excusez-moi

sorry/I'm very sorry	ismahlee/ ana asif	pardon/je suis désolé
let's go	nimsheeyoo	on y va
go away	imshee	va t'en
I don't understand	mafahemsh	je ne comprends pas
do you speak English? (m/f)	takelem/ takelmna ingleesi?	parlez-vous anglais?

Getting around

where's...?	fayn...?	où est...?
the airport	el matar	l'aeroport
the train station	mahattat el tren	la gare de train
the bus station	mahattat el car	la gare routière
the bank	el bank	le banque
the hospital	el mostashfa	l'hôpital
near/far (from here)	qurayab/baeed (min huna)	près/loin (d'ici)
left	liseer	à gauche
right	limeen	à droit
straight ahead	neeshan	tout droit
here	hina	ici
there	hinak	là

Accommodation

hotel	funduq	hôtel
do you have a room?	kayn beet?	avez-vous une chambre?
two beds	jooj tlik	deux lits
one big bed	wahad tlik kebir	un grand lit
shower	doosh	douche
hot water	maa skhoona	eau chaud
can I see?	mumkin ashoofha?	je peux le voir?
key	sarut	clé

Shopping

I (don't) want...	ena (mish) bgheet...	je (ne) veux (pas)...
how much (money)?	shahal (flooss)?	combien (d'argent)?
(that's) expensive	(hada) ghalee	(c'est) cher

Numbers

0	sifr	zéro
1	wahad	un
2	jooj	deux
3	tlata	trois
4	arbaa	quatre
5	khamsa	cinq
6	sitta	six
7	sebaa	sept
8	temanya	huit
9	tisaoud	neuf
10	ashra	dix
11	hadashar	onze
12	etnashar	douze
13	talatashar	treize
14	arbatashar	quatorze
15	khamstashar	quinze
16	sittashar	seize
17	sebatashar	dix-sept
18	tamantashar	dix-huit
19	tisatashar	dix-neuf
20	ashreen	vingt
21	wahad wa ashreen	vingt-et-un
22	jooj wa ashreen	vingt-deux
30	talateen	trente
40	arbaeen	quarante
50	khamseen	cinqante
60	sitteen	soixante
70	sabaeen	soixante-dix
80	tamaneen	quatre vingts
90	tisaeen	quatre-vingt-dix
100	mia	cent
121	mia wa wahad wa ashreen	cent vingt-et-un
200	miateen	deux cents
300	tolta mia	trois cents
1000	alf	mille
a half	nuss	demi
a quarter	roba	quart

Days and times

Monday	nahar el it neen	lundi
Tuesday	nahar et telat	mardi
Wednesday	nahar el arbaa	mercredi

Thursday	nahar el khemis	jeudi
Friday	nahar el jemaa	vendredi
Saturday	nahar es sabt	samedi
Sunday	nahar el had	dimanche
yesterday	imbarih	hier
today	el yoom	aujourd'hui
tomorrow	gheda	demain
what time is it?	shahal fisa'a?	quelle heure est-il?
one o'clock	sa'a wahda	une heure
2.15	jooj wa roba	deux heures et quart
3.30	tlata wa nuss	trois heures et demi
4.45	arbaa ila roba	cinq heures moins quart

Food and drink basics

restaurant	mataam	restaurant
breakfast	iftar	petit déjeuner
egg	beyd	oeuf
butter	zibda	beurre
jam	marmalad	confiture
cheese	jibna	fromage
yoghurt	rayeb	yaourt
salad	salata	salade
olives	zitoun	olives
bread	khobz	pain
salt	melha	sel
pepper	haroor	piment
(without) sugar	(bilesh) sukkar	(sans) sucre
the bill	el hisab	l'addition
fork	forshaat	fourchette
knife	mooss	couteau
spoon	mielaqa	cuillère
plate	tabseel	assiete

Meat, poultry and fish

meat	lahem	viande
beef	baqri	boeuf
chicken	djaj	poulet
lamb	houli	mouton
liver	kibda	foie
pigeon	hamam	pigeon
fish	hout	poisson
prawns	qambri	crevettes

Vegetables

vegetables	khadrawat	légumes
artichoke	qoq	artichaut
aubergine	badinjan	aubergine
beans	loobia	haricots
onions	basal	oignons
potatoes	batata	patates
tomatoes	mateesha	tomates

Fruits and nuts

almonds	looz	amandes
apple	tufah	pomme
banana	banan	banane
dates	tmer	dattes
figs	kermooss	figues
grapes	ainab	raisins
lemon	limoon	limon
melon	battikh	melon
orange	limoon	orange
pomegranate	rooman	granade
prickly pear (cactus fruit)	hendiya	figues de Barbarie
strawberry	frowla	fraise
watermelon	dellah	pastèque

Beverages

water	maa	de l'eau
mineral water	Sidi Ali/Sidi Harazem (brand names)	eau minérale
ice	jeleedi	glace
ice cream	glace	glace
milk	haleeb	lait
coffee	qahwa	café
coffee with a little milk	nuss nuss	café cassé
coffee with plenty of milk	qahwa bi haleeb	café au lait/ café crème
tea (with mint/ wormwood)	atay (bi nana /bi sheeba)	thé (à la menthe/ à l'absinthe)
juice	aseer	jus
beer	birra	bière
wine	sharab	vin
orange juice	aseer limoon	jus d'orange
mixed fruit milkshake	–	jus panache

LANGUAGE

Common dishes and foods

bisara	thick pea soup, usually served with olive oil and cumin
chakchouka	a vegetable stew not unlike ratatouille, though sometimes containing meat or eggs
couscous aux sept legumes	seven-vegetable couscous (often made with meat stock)
harira	bean soup, also usually containing pasta and meat
kefta	minced meat (usually lamb)
loobia	bean stew
mechoui	roast lamb
merguez	small, spicy dark red sausages. usually grilled over charcoal
pastilla	sweet pigeon or chicken pie with cinnamon and filo pastry; a speciality of Fez
(pommes) frites	French fries
salade Marocaine	salad of tomato and cucumber, finely chopped
tajine	a Moroccan casserole cooked over charcoal in a thick ceramic bowl with a conical lid
tanjia	a Marrakshi speciality, jugged beef – the term in fact refers to the jug

Breads and pastries

briouats/ doits de Fatima	sweet filo pastry with a savoury filling, a bit like a miniature pastilla
briouats au miel	sweet filo pastry envelopes filled with nuts and honey
cornes de gazelles (Fr.)/kab el ghazal (Ar.)	marzipan-filled, banana-shaped pastry horns
harsha	flat, leavened griddle bread with a gritty crust, served at cafés for breakfast

millefeuille	custard slice
msimmen	flat griddle bread made from dough sprinkled with oil, rolled out and folded over several times, rather like an Indian paratha

Common local terms

kif kif/ p'hal p'hal	same thing (I don't mind which)
makaynsh mooshkil	no problem
sidi	sir, monsieur

Glossary

bab	gate or door
babouche	traditional slipper
chaabi	Moroccan popular music (usually folk-derived)
dar	house or palace
darj w ktarf	(literally, "cheek and shoulder") Almohad architectural design resembling fleur-de-lys
gandora	men's cotton garment (equivalent to a kaftan)
ginbri	African lute
jebel	mountain(s)
koubba	dome, and by extension, a tomb with a dome (usually belonging to a marabout)
marabout	Sufi saint
mihrab	niche in the Mecca-facing wall of a mosque indicating the direction of prayer
moussem	popular local festival
souk	market
tadelakt	super-smooth waterproof plaster glaze traditionally used in hammams
thuya	aromatic mahogany-like hardwood from the trunk and rootstock of a Moroccan cypress tree
zaouia	Sufi sanctuary (usually around the tomb of a marabout)
zellij	geometrical tilework

SMALL PRINT

Publishing information

This fourth edition published April 2018 by **Rough Guides Ltd**, Alpha House, 100 Borough High Street, London, SE1 1LB

Distribution

UK, Ireland and Europe
Apa Publications (UK) Ltd; sales@roughguides.com
United States and Canada
Ingram Publisher Services; ips@ingramcontent.com
Australia and New Zealand
Woodslane; info@woodslane.com.au
Southeast Asia
Apa Publications (SN) Pte; sales@roughguides.com
Worldwide
Apa Publications (UK) Ltd; sales@roughguides.com

Special sales, content licensing and co-publishing
Rough Guides can be purchased in bulk quantities at discounted prices. We can create special editions, personalized jackets and corporate imprints tailored to your needs. sales@roughguides.com
roughguides.com
Printed in China

All rights reserved
© 2018 Apa Digital AG and Rough Guides Ltd
No part of this book may be reproduced in any form without permission from the publisher except for the quotation of brief passages in reviews.

136pp includes index
A catalogue record for this book is available from the British Library
ISBN 978-0-241-30649-9
The publishers and authors have done their best to ensure the accuracy and currency of all the information in **Pocket Rough Guide Marrakesh**, however, they can accept no responsibility for any loss, injury, or inconvenience sustained by any traveller as a result of information or advice contained in the guide.
1 3 5 7 9 8 6 4 2

Rough Guides credits

Updater: Daniel Jacobs
Editor: Alice Park
Layout: Anita Singh
Cartography: Richard Marchi, Katie Bennett and Ed Wright
Picture editor: Phoebe Lowndes
Proofreader: Emma Beatson
Managing editor: Keith Drew
Cover photo research: Nicole Newman
Original design: Richard Czapnik

Help us update

We've gone to a lot of effort to ensure that the fourth edition of the **Pocket Rough Guide Marrakesh** is accurate and up-to-date. However, things change – places get "discovered", opening hours are notoriously fickle, restaurants and rooms raise prices or lower standards. If you feel we've got it wrong or left something out, we'd like to know, and if you can remember the address, the price, the hours, the phone number, so much the better.

Please send your comments with the subject line "**Pocket Rough Guide Marrakesh Update**" to mail@roughguides.com. We'll credit all contributions and send a copy of the next edition (or any other Rough Guide if you prefer) for the very best emails.

Photo credits

All photos © Rough Guides except the following:
(Key: t-top; c-centre; b-bottom; l-left; r-right)

Cover: Koutoubia Mosque **Getty Images:** Photolibrary / Visions Of Our Land
Cover flap: Traditional house in the Medina **SuperStock:** Age Fotostock (t). Ben Youssef Medersa **SuperStock:** Pixtal (c). Café Arabe **Alamy Stock Photo:** LOOK Die Bildagentur der Fotografen GmbH (b)

1 Getty Images: Robert Harding / Matthew Williams-Ellis
2 Robert Harding: Image Broker / Fabian Von Poser (t). **4Corners Images:** Richard Taylor (cr). **Alamy Stock Photo:** Funkyfood London-Paul Williams (br). **Alamy Stock Photo:** Giuseppe Masci (bl)
4 Axiom: Timothy Allen
6 Alamy Stock Photo: Fahim Abdelmajid (t). **Getty Images:** Herve Hughes (b)
10 Getty Images: Photographer's Choice / Marco Brivio
11 Getty Images: Anadolu Agency / Jalal Morchidi (t). **SuperStock** (t)
12 Alamy Stock Photo: Luis Dafos (t)
13 4Corners Images: SIME / Alessandro Saffo (t). **Alamy Stock Photo:** Travelib prime (b)
14 SuperStock: Giovanni Mereghetti (t). **Alamy Stock Photo:** World Pictures / Avalon (b)
15 SuperStock (t)
16 Alamy Stock Photo: Hemis (t). Elan Fleisher (b)
17 SuperStock: Christian Kober (b)
18 Getty Images: Robert Harding / Emanuele Ciccomartino (c)
20 SuperStock: CINTRACT Romain (t)
22 Alamy Stock Photo: Bartosz

Luczak (t). **Picfair:** Monti (c)
23 Alamy Stock Photo: Funkyfood London-Paul Williams (t). **Alamy Stock Photo:** AGF Srl (b)
24–25 Getty Images: Hemis.fr RM / ESCUDERO Patrick
46 Alamy Stock Photo: Joanne Moyes
47 La Qoubba Galerie d'Art: Amine Rhefir (b)
51 Nomad (t)
57 Alamy Stock Photo: AA World Travel Library
59 Entreprise Bouchaib Complexe D'Artisanat: Paola Vedovati
61 Café Clock: Azeddine Zitsu
66 Getty Images: Photographer's Choice / Peter Phipp
68 Marilynn Taylor
72 Amal Restaurant Solidaire
73 Grand Café de la Poste
76 Alamy Stock Photo: Stephen Barnes
77 Kechmara: Arnaud Foltran
78 Alamy Stock Photo: LOOK Die Bildagentur der Fotografen GmbH
79 Hotel Sofitel Marrakech Lounge and Spa
80 Alamy Photo Stock: Pontino
83 Kasbah du Toubkal
84 Alamy Stock Photo: Images & Stories
88 Alamy Stock Photo: Nick Hanna
89 Alamy Stock Photo: LH Images
90 Galerie d'art Frédéric Damgaard: Daniel Jacobs
91 Alamy Stock Photo: Danita Delimont
92 Alamy Stock Photo: imageBROKER
93 Alamy Stock Photo: Nicholas Pitt
94–95 Riad Houdou
110–111 AWL Images: Peter Adams

Index

Maps are marked in **bold**.

INDEX

ROUGH GUIDES

Start your journey at roughguides.com

Ebooks | Expert destination coverage | Inspiring articles
Beautiful galleries | Videos, competitions, quizzes and more

Sign up to the monthly **newsletter** for all the latest from Rough Guides

Long bus journey?
Phone run out of juice?

☞ **TEST YOUR KNOWLEDGE** WITH OUR ROUGH GUIDES TRAVEL QU

1 Denim, the pencil, the stethoscope and the hot-air balloon were all invented in which country?

   a. Italy   c. Germany
   b. France   d. Switzerland

2 What is the busiest airport in the world?

   a. London Heathrow   c. Chicago O'Hare
   b. Tokyo International   d. Hartsfield-Jackson
                                  Atlanta International

3 Which of these countries does not have the equator running through it?

   a. Brazil   b. Tanzania
   c. Indonesia   d. Colombia

4 What is the principal religion of Japan?

   a. Confucianism   c. Jainism
   b. Buddhism   d. Shinto

5 Every July in Sonkajärvi, central Finland, contestants gather for the World Championships of which sport?

   a. Zorbing   c. Chess-boxing
   b. Wife-carrying   d. Extreme ironing

6 What colour are post boxes in Germany?

   a. Red   c. Blue
   b. Green   d. Yellow

7 For three days each April during Songkran festival in Thailand, people take to the streets to throw what at each other?

   a. Water   c. Tomatoes
   b. Oranges   d. Underwear